LNER Steam Revival

What the preserved steam locomotives of the LNER lack in quantity they certainly make up for in quality, with achievements reflecting those of their days in service.

LNER A4 Pacifics Nos. 4464 *Bittern* and 4468 *Mallard*, A2 No. 60532 *Blue Peter* and V2 2-6-2 No. 4771 *Green Arrow* line up at Barrow Hill Roundhouse.

The London & North Eastern Railway was the railway company that served the eastern half of England and Scotland, north of London, after the Grouping of the independent railway companies in 1923. It was formed by the amalgamation mainly of the Great Northern Railway, North Eastern Railway, Great Central Railway, Great Eastern Railway, North British Railway and Great North of Scotland Railway.

Apple green engines, teak coaches, the 'Flying Scotsman', the most intensive steam-worked suburban service in the world, streamlined A4 Pacifics, long lumbering coal trains heading for London, but also quaint rural byways, these are the images conjured up by memories of the LNER.

King's Cross, Stoke Bank, Doncaster 'Plant', Woodhead Tunnel, Stainmore Summit and Belah Viaduct, the Newcastle flat crossing, the Royal Border Bridge, Glenfinnan viaduct and Whitrope Summit; the newly formed railway company inherited some iconic railway infrastructure, but also some quite ancient motive power and rolling stock. Much of its terrain was relatively flat, apart from lines that penetrated some way into the Pennines and the Yorkshire Moors, but north of the border, this all changed. The Aberdeen road, the Waverley route and especially the West Highland line, were some of the toughest routes in the country and needed a special breed of locomotive and crews to handle them.

Never the most profitable of the Big Four, its innovation and high-speed exploits are all the more remarkable for this, and it could be argued that more effort should have been made to make rural routes and goods services more profitable.

On Nationalisation, the English portion of the LNER was broken up into the Eastern and North Eastern regions of British Railways, while its Scottish routes were combined with those of the LMS to form the Scottish Region.

In preservation, LNER engines have continued to outshine their competitors, with the accent more on quality than quantity. Being directly descended from the Stockton & Darlington Railway, which has

celebrated its anniversary every 50 years, the LNER inherited a concern for its heritage and very much pioneered 'official' preservation, not having scrapped any engines once classed as preserved, as was the case with the GWR and LMS. It opened Britain's first railway museum, which even became the home for the first publicly preserved engines from two of the other 'Big Four' companies; it operated the first preserved engine to haul a main line passenger train, and after Nationalisation in 1948, the first preserved locomotives to run on BR were two ex-GNR Atlantics brought out of York museum to run on the GN main line out of King's Cross.

The first privately preserved steam engine to haul a main line railtour was a GNR one, Captain Smith's J52 No. 1247, and when the private preservation of main line steam locomotives started in earnest in the early 1960s, it was not only A3 Pacific No. 4472 *Flying Scotsman* but also K4 2-6-0 No. 3442 *The Great Marquess* which pioneered preserved main line express steam operation, followed by three of the celebrated LNER A4 streamlined Pacifics, Nos. 60009 *Union of South Africa*, 60019 *Bittern* and 4498 *Sir Nigel Gresley*. To put this into perspective, two privately preserved GWR Castles briefly saw main line use in the 1960s but no privately preserved engines of either SR or LMS origin.

Such was the interest among private and overseas buyers in acquiring streamlined A4 Pacifics for preservation, that the only class of 'Big Four' Pacific to be rendered extinct at the end of steam was the Peppercorn A1, yet in 2008, when a new Class 8 Pacific took to the rails, it was to an LNER design, *Tornado* was born and a big gap in steam preservation was filled – and in some style, with A1 No. 60163 finally proving that it could more than match an A4 any day, and has challenged *Flying Scotsman's* claim to be the most famous steam locomotive in the world.

This book tells the story of each of the one-time LNER or LNER-designed steam locomotives which have survived, 36 of which have steamed in preservation since 1948. ∎

Editor:
Brian Sharpe

Designer:
Leanne Lawrence

Reprographics:
Jonathan Schofield & Lorna Herbert

Senior sub-editor:
Dan Sharp

Production manager:
Craig Lamb

Publisher:
Tim Hartley

Publishing director:
Dan Savage

Commercial director:
Nigel Hole

Published by:
Mortons Media Group Ltd,
Media Centre,
Morton Way,
Horncastle,
Lincolnshire
LN9 6JR
Tel: 01507 529529

ISBN:
978-1-909128-63-7

GER J17 0-6-0 No. 8217 meets A1 Pacific No. 60163 *Tornado* at Barrow Hill.

COVER IMAGE
MAIN IMAGE: Only a year old, No. 60163 *Tornado* departs from Goathland on the North Yorkshire Moors Railway in May 2009.

LNER A4 Pacific No. 60019 *Bittern* departs from Grosmont on the North Yorkshire Moors Railway as classmate No. 60009 *Union of South Africa* awaits its next duty in March 2008.

LNER K1 2-6-0 No. 62005, B1 4-6-0 No. 61264, K4 2-6-0 No. 61994 *The Great Marquess* and GER J15 0-6-0 No. 65462 line up round the turntable at Barrow Hill Roundhouse on November 10, 2007. FRED KERR

Contents

An apple green doubleheader as LNER V2 2-6-2 No. 4771 *Green Arrow* and B1 4-6-0 No. 1306 *Mayflower* depart from Peterborough Nene Valley in September 2007.

CHAPTER I

LNER heritage lines

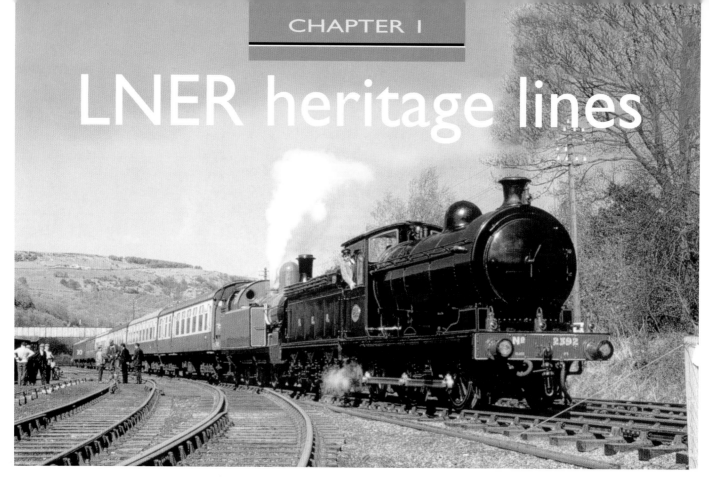

ABOVE: NER P3 0-6-0 No. 2392 and Lambton Colliery 0-6-2T No. 29 head the Royal Train marking the reopening of the North Yorkshire Moors Railway by The Duchess of Kent, into Grosmont on May 1, 1973.
JOHN M BOYES

A remarkable selection of lines of all varieties from constituent companies of the LNER have been saved and turned into heritage railways.

Two of the country's premier preserved railways are the North Yorkshire Moors Railway, the most popular in Britain, and the Great Central Railway, Britain's only double-track steam railway. The GNR though is perhaps poorly represented in terms of operating lengths of heritage line in comparison with the GCR, NER, GER and even the Scottish companies.

North Yorkshire Moors Railway

Britain's most popular preserved steam railway is an LNER one, engineered by George Stephenson and once part of the North Eastern Railway.

The Whitby & Pickering Railway was built in an attempt to halt Whitby's decline as a port. After the success of the Stockton & Darlington Railway, the possibility of a railway from Whitby to either Stockton or Pickering was considered and in 1832 George Stephenson was asked to report on the two routes. His report favoured a horse-worked railway to Pickering, the intention being to continue the line to York and beyond.

The line from Grosmont to Pickering opened on June 8, 1835. George Hudson's York & North Midland Railway took over the W&P and converted it to a double-track steam railway before it was absorbed into the North Eastern Railway in 1854.

By the early 1860s the NER had opened a deviation line, which included a new station at Goathland, on July 1, 1865.

The line eventually became part of a mostly double-track through route from York to Whitby and carried heavy holiday traffic especially on summer Saturdays.

Local services to Whitby were operated by DMUs from 1959 and diesel locomotives gradually replaced steam on the few longer-distance trains, but the Beeching Report in 1963 recommended the closure of the remaining three railways serving Whitby. The Esk Valley branch line to Middlesbrough did survive but on March 8, 1965, the Malton-Whitby line and the coast line to Scarborough were closed.

A heritage trust was set up in 1967 and members gradually obtained access to the line with permission to carry out maintenance and run occasional members-only steam galas, ultimately reopening in 1973. At peak times, Grosmont is claimed to be the second busiest station in North Yorkshire, after York,

with services now also running over part of Network Rail's Esk Valley line into Whitby.

Great Central Railway

Britain's only preserved double-track main line heritage railway was also once part of the LNER. The Manchester Sheffield & Lincolnshire Railway was built to move coal and other goods across the Pennines through Woodhead tunnel.

But Edward Watkin, who became chairman of the MSLR in 1864, had ambitions for the line to be linked with continental Europe via a channel tunnel. Having progressed the MSLR as far south as Annesley, the only gap was between there and Quainton Road on the Metropolitan Railway, which he also happened to be chairman of.

Construction of what became known as the London Extension started in 1894 and the line was opened on March 9, 1899, with a new London terminus being built at Marylebone. The MSLR had become the Great Central Railway in 1897. However, little other progress had been made towards Watkin's grand vision of an ultimate Manchester to Paris route via a channel tunnel.

The GCR became part of the LNER in 1923 and nationalisation in 1948 saw it becoming part of the Eastern Region of BR, which was geographically inappropriate and so, in 1958, the GCR lines were transferred to the London Midland Region where it simply duplicated other LMR main lines, leading to its inevitable decline. Through expresses were withdrawn in 1960 and in 1966 the line closed as a through route to London and was lifted south of Rugby. Until 1969, a DMU service ran from Rugby to Nottingham.

By this time, two or three standard gauge branch lines had been reopened by volunteers as preserved steam railways. With BR having banned the use of preserved steam engines on its main lines, a group of enthusiasts came up with the ambitious idea of preserving a section of the GCR main line for running main line steam engines at main line speeds.

The Main Line Preservation Group, later the Main Line Steam Trust, met with only moderate success altough it did commence running regular services from Loughborough as far as Rothley in 1973.

The Great Central Railway (1976) Ltd was formed to raise funds through the sale of shares. Even then only the single track from Loughborough to Rothley was saved but Charnwood Borough Council purchased the land from Loughborough Central

LEFT: Running on double track, GCR O4 2-8-0 No. 63601 approaches Quorn & Woodhouse with a goods train as a passenger train departs for Loughborough.

station to Belgrave & Birstall. The present-day Great Central Railway now runs from Loughborough Central through to Leicester North close to Belgrave & Birstall.

Volunteers completing the reinstatement of double track from Loughborough Central to Rothley stands as one of the biggest achievements of the railway preservation movement. Initially the dream of one-time GCR president David Clarke, the double track was inaugurated on June 1, 2000, by LNER V2 2-6-2 No. 60800 *Green Arrow*. The GCR offers the authentic spectacle of a double-track main line railway, although the ambition of running passenger trains at main line speeds in excess of the statutory maximum of 25mph for heritage railways has not yet been realised.

Great Central Railway (Nottingham)

At the same time as the GCR London Extension closed in 1969, the Ministry of Defence depot at Ruddington, south of Nottingham, closed, and British Gypsum ceased to use the Loughborough-East Leake section for gypsum traffic.

After the formation of the GCR Northern Development Association, Rushcliffe Borough Council agreed to lease part of the former MoD site at Ruddington to the association. Plans were made for a heritage centre, which is on the branch line off the Great Central Railway (Nottingham) consisting of approximately 10 miles of the former GCR main line running north from Loughborough where it connects with the Midland Main Line.

Network Rail had originally severed the line north of East Leake so that it could continue to route freight trains on to the line., so the GCR(N) was unable to access Rushcliffe Halt. Ironically, it was British Gypsum's intentions to renew rail traffic that finally allowed the GCR(N) to buy the line and restore it initially for freight use, with gypsum trains running during the week and the GCR(N) operating heritage trains at the weekend.

Regular services to Rushcliffe Halt were started in 2003, and passenger trains further south now run on a regular basis to the site of a proposed Loughborough High Level station. The railway is currently not connected to the Great Central Railway itself although the GCR has plans to reunite the two preserved lines, by reinstating the bridge over the Midland Main Line just south of Loughborough Midland station.

Reconnecting both preserved sections will create an 18-mile-long heritage main line, from the outskirts of Nottingham to the outskirts of Leicester. However, while the gap is relatively short, and work has started on reinstating the bridge, the rest of the engineering work will still be a multi-million-pound project and likely to take many years.

North Norfolk Railway

THE Midland & Great Northern Joint Railway remained independent at the Grouping and only became part of the LNER in 1937. Never profitable, virtually the entire system closed in February 1959.

In October of that year, the Midland & Great Northern Joint Railway Society was founded, being one of the first railway preservation groups in the UK. Its founder members had the initial intention of preserving as much of the system as they could, buying two main line engines and some stock. However, it was not until much of the last-surviving M&GN branch line from Sheringham to Melton Constable closed in 1964 that the society decided on preserving the section of line between Sheringham and Weybourne.

The line is now just over five miles long and work on rebuilding it started in 1965 after the launch of operating company North Norfolk Railway plc. Two years later on June 4 the two steam locomotives, GER J15 0-6-0 No. 65462 and LNER B12 4-6-0 No. 61572, were delivered to Sheringham by rail via Cromer, after which the link with BR was severed.

Services commenced to Weybourne in 1975 but BR had lifted the track beyond there and this had to be relaid before services could be extended to a new Holt station from 1987.

Today the North Norfolk Railway represents as much ex-

BELOW: No main line steam locomotives are based on the GCR(N) but there have been many visitors; GER J15 0-6-0 No. 65462 crosses Stanford viaduct over the River Soar just north of the Midland main line at Loughborough on February 22, 2004. GEOFF SILCOCK

RIGHT: GNR N2 0-6-2T
No. 1744 and LNER B1 4-6-0
No. 61306 *Mayflower* arrive
at Yaxham on the Mid-
Norfolk Railway on July 14,
2012.

M&GN mileage in preservation as there is on Network Rail and in 2010 the two remaining five-mile sections of the M&GN were finally reconnected, when the NNR reinstated the level crossing at Sheringham and reconnected it to the national rail network for the first time in 40 years, the occasion being marked by a main line steam railtour from King's Cross to Holt.

Mid-Norfolk Railway

The fifth-longest standard gauge heritage railway in Britain, the MNR, was a relative newcomer to the heritage portfolio, much of its infrastructure having been sold off, and main line steam traction has been a relatively recent innovation.

It is the southern section of the former Wymondham, Dereham, Fakenham and Wells-next-the-Sea line, opened by the Norfolk Railway in 1847, that became part of the Great Eastern Railway in 1862, and which closed to passengers in stages between 1964 and 1969, when the Wymondham-Dereham services were withdrawn, although freight traffic continued as far as North Elmham until June 1989.

The Fakenham and Dereham Railway Society was formed in 1978, with the intention of preserving the line between these two towns. The society established a base at Hardingham station then moved to Yaxham and eventually County School station.

After the announcement of the complete closure of the line, a new company called the Great Eastern Railway (1989) Ltd was created to save it, and was supported by the F&DRS, which changed its name to the Mid Norfolk Railway Society in 1990.

The first passenger train operated at the County School site on November 2, 1991. However, during the early 1990s, the GER (1989) announced plans to lift the railway between Dereham and Wymondham. The MNRS withdrew its support making its own bid for the line.

The GER (1989) started lifting track north of Dereham but a year later it had called in the receivers. In 1994 BR granted the MNRS access between Wymondham and North Elmham.

The Mid-Norfolk Railway Preservation Trust was established in 1995 with the aim of buying and restoring the Wymondham to North Elmham section and on November 29 that year the first diesel-hauled trains ran between Yaxham and the outskirts of Dereham.

The original Dereham station re-opened to passengers on July 26, 1997, with the first services being operated by an industrial saddle tank. The 11-mile Wymondham to Dereham section was purchased by the MNRPT and passenger services between Dereham and Wymondham commenced in 1999, with the opening of Wymondham Abbey station. Services were normally DMU-operated, with the first steam passenger service running on April 30, 2006, headed by WR 0-6-0PT No. 9466.

From 2013, occasional trains run north of Dereham as far as Hoe, much of the track remaining as far as North Elmham, but a mile-long section requires reinstatement before regular services can be extended. The line remains connected with Network Rail at Wymondham, and occasional military trains, railtours and stock movements take place. It remains the long-term aim to reach Fakenham.

Mid-Suffolk Light Railway

The MSLR was not one of the most profitable parts of the LNER empire. Although not the subject of a preservation project until nearly 50 years after closure, it is one of the most authentically recreated, if rather short, preserved railways.

The original Mid-Suffolk Light Railway was an ambitious scheme to open up central Suffolk under he Light Railways Act of 1896. It was intended to run from Haughley Junction on the GER main line, to Halesworth, on the East Suffolk line.

The MSLR opened during September 1908 for passenger traffic, running the 19 miles to Laxfield from Haughley, stopping short of Halesworth. By 1924 it had been absorbed into the LNER and was busy for a while but closure was announced and the final train ran on July 26, 1952.

As late as 1990, a small group of enthusiasts felt that there ought to be a permanent reminder of the line and so a museum was set up in the village of Wetheringsett, almost on the site of the former Brockford station.

The first trains operated in early July 2002, exactly 50 years after closure, with two GER coaches headed by newly overhauled GER Y14 0-6-0 No. 564 from the North Norfolk Railway.

Epping Ongar Railway

In 1856 the Eastern Counties Railway, which later became part of the GER, opened a line from Stratford to Loughton, extended to Ongar in 1865.

The London Passenger Transport Board, later to become London Transport (LT), was established in 1933. In 1948 an extension to the Central line reached Loughton, with a steam shuttle continuing from Loughton to serve Ongar.

Following Nationalisation in 1948, as the line from Leyton to Loughton was served by LT, the line was transferred to the London Transport Executive, and the electrified Central line was extended to Epping in 1949, after which the LTE also took control of the line to Ongar, and hired the steam shuttle from BR.

During the 1950s it was eventually decided to electrify the Ongar line 'on the cheap', but steam freight trains continued.

LT eventually closed the Ongar section on September 30, 1994, but Pilot Developments purchased the Epping to Ongar line with the intention of running trains but never did. However, the Epping Ongar Railway Volunteer Society was formed to repair

and preserve the neglected buildings and track. Working alongside the owners, the volunteer group gradually restored the line and station building at Ongar so that trains could run once again and provide a passenger service to North Weald. On October 10, 2004, the first EORVS DMU service left Ongar.

After a change in the line's ownership in late 2007, it was decided to cease running trains and to concentrate on improving the infrastructure to enable locomotive-hauled trains to run again.

The preservation project had gone through a lot of problems and false starts but finally opened for serious business in 2012, back in its GER condition. The trackwork through the stations was renewed and realigned, to make it the correct height for the platforms and also to reinstate the original track layout, all the ongoing infrastructure improvements being with the aim to run trains to connect at Epping once more.

Tanfield Railway

A line which has always been associated with industrial motive power was built by the Brandling Junction Railway and became part of the NER. However, part of the route is very much older and enables the Tanfield Railway to claim to be the oldest railway in the world still running trains on its original route.

It runs on part of a former colliery wooden waggonway, for three miles from East Tanfield to Sunniside, Gateshead. The intermediate station, Andrews House, is situated near to Marley Hill engine shed.

The Tanfield Railway was originally built to transport coal to staithes on the River Tyne for loading on to boats. The oldest part of the original waggonway, located to the north east of the present heritage line, in the Lobley Hill area, dates from 1647, but the route and structures of the oldest section of the now-preserved part of the line, between Sunniside and Causey, date from 1725, and so the Tanfield claims to be the world's oldest working railway.

Conversion of the horse-drawn waggonway to a conventional railway began in 1837, and by 1881 it was converted to steam locomotive operation, becoming part of the NER. Locomotives were stabled at Bowes Bridge near Sunniside, at the top of a rope-worked incline which ran from the staithes near Gateshead. East Tanfield Colliery closed in 1964, and the railway, by this time owned by the National Coal Board, was closed and the track lifted.

Marley Hill engine shed was built in 1854 by the Pontop & Jarrow Railway, later known as the Bowes Railway, which crossed the NER's Tanfield branch on the level. The early years of the railway as a preservation project concentrated on Marley Hill and when the line was reopened a curve was installed to connect the shed area to the Tanfield branch for the first time.

Passenger trains from Marley Hill to Sunniside started running on July 2, 1981, and the first train south to East Tanfield ran on October 18, 1992.

Marley Hill, believed to be the oldest operational locomotive

shed in the world, remained open until 1970. The line's locomotive stock is industrial, mainly Tyneside-built and the carriage stock mostly vintage four-wheelers, but small main line locomotives are seen on gala weekends, and the regular coal trains are a unique feature of steam preservation.

Lincolnshire Wolds Railway

The GNR has been disproportionately represented in the history of active preservation by its locomotives and their achievements, but the LWR is the only substantial part of the GNR to see regular heritage-era steam passenger trains.

The East Lincolnshire Railway line opened for passenger traffic on March 1, 1848, from Grimsby to Louth and was extended southwards, operated by the GNR, becoming its main line from Grimsby to Peterborough on the ECML.

Most intermediate stations between Grimsby and Louth closed on September 11, 1961, and passenger services ceased completely on October 5, 1970, but the line remained open for freight from Grimsby to Louth until December 1980.

The Grimsby-Louth Group was formed to fight the closure of the line and became the Grimsby-Louth Railway Preservation Society, whose original goal was to preserve the 14-mile Grimsby to Louth line, centred on Ludborough where the operating base was set up in 1984. The signalbox was rebuilt in original GN-style and trains started running north from Ludborough on an occasional basis with the line gradually being extended.

Tracklaying continued in the direction of North Thoresby and 2009 saw the first passenger train arrive in the village's newly reopened station. Motive power has been predominantly industrial but with occasional main line visitors.

ABOVE: Re-creating the last train of 1952, GER J15 0-6-0 No. 65462 running as No. 65447 stands at Brockford & Wetheringsett station on the Mid-Suffolk Light Railway with two GER coaches on July 27, 2002.

BELOW: NER P3 0-6-0 No. 2392 at Stanhope on the opening day of the Weardale Railway in July 2004.

ABOVE: LNER B1 4-6-0 No. 1306 *Mayflower* passes Longueville Junction on the Nene Valley Railway. The track to the left is the Great Northern Railway's Fletton branch which connects the NVR with the East Coast Main Line.

RIGHT: Metropolitan Railway E class 0-4-4T No. 1 arrives at North Weald on the Epping Ongar Railway with Metropolitan stock during the railway's first steam gala on June 30, 2013.

Stainmore Railway and Eden Valley Railway

Kirkby Stephen East station on the South Durham & Lancashire Union Railway between Barnard Castle and Tebay opened to passenger traffic on August 8, 1861, and became part of the Stockton & Darlington Railway, later the NER. It closed to passengers in 1962 but the line stayed open for freight until 1974. The site was purchased by Stainmore Properties Ltd In 1997 after it had been used as a bobbin factory, and Stainmore Railway Company volunteers have worked over the years to develop a heritage centre and an operational railway.

The station had an extensive goods yard, an engine shed, carriage shed and turntable, and saw long-distance excursions in its heyday.

August 2011 marked the 150th anniversary of the railway, and to commemorate this, steam-hauled passenger services operated on a short length of line. A short distance to the north, the Eden Valley Railway operates DMU passenger services out of Warcop, the line from here to Appleby having previously been retained for military traffic.

Nene Valley Railway

The NVR's main running line from Peterborough to Yarwell Mill was built by the London & Birmingham Railway, later part of the London & North Western Railway, but a branch from Longueville Junction, which now forms the line's connection with Network Rail, was built by the GNR.

NER Y7 0-4-0T No. 68088 at Ludborough on the Lincolnshire Wolds Railway on June 15, 2003. PAUL APPLETON

NER-designed J72 0-6-0T No. 69023 passes Terrace Junction with a coal train on the Tanfield Railway.

The L&BR line was opened from Blisworth on the West Coast Main Line to Peterborough in 1845, making an end on connection with the Eastern Counties Railway, and briefly formed the city's rail link with the capital until the GNR line from King's Cross was opened. There was initially no direct connection between the LBR and GNR but a 1¼-mile loop line was built by the GNR which has seen more closures and reopenings than most. It has always formed a valuable main line link for the NVR but has only recently been finally secured, and steam-worked brakevan shuttles now occasionally operate as well as incoming railtours and other stock movements.

Weardale Railway
Originally running from Bishop Auckland to Wearhead in County Durham over a distance of 25 miles, the Weardale Railway was built as far as Frosterley in 1844-47, becoming part of the Stockton & Darlington Railway in 1857, and extended to Stanhope in 1862. The final extension to Wearhead was opened by the NER in 1895.

Passenger services ceased in 1953, leaving only freight services to Eastgate. However, Durham County Council promoted occasional passenger trains after 1983 and this became a scheduled weekend-only summer service in 1988-92, while a daily train continued to serve Eastgate cement works.

In March 1993, though Lafarge decided to switch to road transport and the line closed, the Weardale Railway preservation project was set up to run a steam service on the scenic western section.

The Weardale Railway Trust's members were supporters of the preservation project. Large sums of public sector finance were obtained or pledged from various sources and a 40-strong workforce was recruited, with a depot and an operations base established at Wolsingham, with the station at Stanhope being restored. Steam services started in July 2004, using NELPG's NER P3 0-6-0 No. 2392 and Tanfield's Austerity 0-6-0ST No. 49.

The project proved impossibly over-ambitious and perhaps inevitably suffered cash flow difficulties; in 2005 the company was placed in administration. It was apparently saved by the intervention of a community interest company known as Ealing Community Transport, which allowed Weardale Railways Ltd to resume limited services on the line in August 2006; normally DMU operated, as steam services have never run regularly for any length of time.

But then in 2008, ECT needed to relinquish its railway operations, which were all bought by a US company, Iowa Pacific Holdings, through a new British company, British American Rail Services.

Long-term salvation for the line only came in December 2009, when it was announced that UK Coal was intending to transport coal from an opencast mine nearby, guaranteeing the line's future. There was much local opposition and steam tourist services inevitably took a back seat but Network Rail completed

the connection to the main line system at Bishop Auckland in early September 2009.

In February 2010, a King's Cross to Stanhope railtour became the first main line passenger service to travel the line since the 1990s, and was followed by occasional steam-hauled railtours to Stanhope.

Regular passenger services to Bishop Auckland started on May 23, 2010, and the first loaded coal train left Wolsingham on June 16, 2011, bound for Scunthorpe steelworks. The line currently runs 18 miles from Bishop Auckland to Eastgate, making it the fourth longest preserved standard gauge railway in Great Britain. Regular services to Bishop Auckland have ceased as they were poorly patronised and the railway now runs only occasional diesel-hauled passenger services.

Wensleydale Railway
The 40-mile Wensleydale Railway was built in stages during the 19th century and connected the East Coast main line at Northallerton with the Settle & Carlisle line at Garsdale. It closed to passenger services in stages in the 1950s-60s.

Eighteen miles of track were lifted between Redmire and Garsdale, but stone traffic from Redmire quarry to the British Steel plant at Redcar continued to travel on the remaining 22 miles from Northallerton to Redmire until December 18, 1992.

It was the 1989 reprieve of the Settle & Carlisle line which led to the formation of the Wensleydale Railway Association in 1990, with the aim of running passenger services on the surviving 22-mile section, while the campaign continued for the reconstruction of the 18-mile missing link.

In 2000, the WRA formed a Wensleydale Railway plc, which launched a share offer to raise funds and more than £1.2 million was raised.

The company leased the line from Network Rail in 2003 and DMU services began on July 4, 2003, over the 12-mile section between Leeming Bar and Leyburn, extended to Redmire in 2004. Services are aimed at commuters and shoppers as well as tourists.

With the connection still in place at Northallerton, occasional railtours visit the line, sometimes steam-hauled, and regular steam services are now operated in the summer season and at Christmas. It is planned to run regular services into Northallerton in the near future and eventually extend the railway westwards towards Aysgarth Falls.

Derwent Valley Railway
The Derwent Valley Light Railway came into existence as a result of the Light Railways Act of 1896 which made railway building easier, but it was not until 1912 that construction began after difficulties in raising the capital required.

The line ran from Layerthorpe, on the NER's Foss Islands branch east of York, to Cliff Common on the North Eastern Railway's line between Selby and Market Weighton. The southern end of the line from Wheldrake to Cliff Common was opened to

ABOVE: LNER K1 2-6-0 No. 62005 passes Bedale on the Wensleydale Railway with the North Eastern Locomotive Preservation Group's 'Three Dales' railtour on May 12, 2007.

goods traffic on October 29, 1912, and on July 19, 1913, the whole line was opened.

The railway remained independent but passenger services ended as early as 1926. The Beeching Report closed the Selby-Market Weighton line in 1964 and this led to the closure of the Cliff Common to Wheldrake section of the still-independent DVR.

Further sections closed but the northern section managed to soldier on, and following the opening of the National Railway Museum in 1975, the DVLR started running a steam passenger service in the summer of 1977, with NER J72 0-6-0T No. 69023. This continued in 1978 but the following year saw reduced passenger numbers and the trains ceased, with freight services ending in 1981 and a farewell special running on September 27, 1981.

However, half a mile of line west of Murton Lane station was taken over by the Yorkshire Museum of Farming, and in 1985, the Light Railway Order was transferred to this section of line. In 1993 the Derwent Valley Railway Preservation Society was given permission to operate under the name of Derwent Valley Light Railway. Trains now operate on summer Sundays over this short section and even the J72 paid a return visit in 2012.

East Anglian Railway Museum

The Stour Valley Railway Preservation Society was formed on September 24, 1968, to preserve the three miles of GER line from Sudbury to Long Melford. Fundraising however was unsuccessful.

But the headquarters of the SVRPS was established at the derelict Chappel and Wakes Colne station on the Marks Tey to

Sudbury section in December 1969, and within three months Hunslet 0-6-0ST *Gunby* worked passenger shuttles in the yard.

A reappraisal of operations was eventually undertaken as the society had obtained a substantial collection of East Anglian railway equipment. It was decided in 1986 to turn the building into the East Anglian Railway Museum.

Steam trains operate on selected weekends and GER N7 0-6-2T No. 69621 is in the society's ownership and has operated at the site occasionally.

Colne Valley Railway

Close to the Stour Valley, the Colne Valley is a privately owned heritage line and rather short but has seen LNER steam in action.

The railway occupies part of the former Colne Valley and Halstead Railway from Birdbrook to Wakes Colne, which opened in stages between 1860 and 1863. This part of the railway was a through line. Passenger services ceased on December 30, 1961, but freight continued until 1965.

The land was purchased in 1973 and the preservation society was formed the following year. The original Sible & Castle Headingham station buildings one mile away were taken down carefully brick by brick and later rebuilt at the new Castle Hedingham station. Industrial steam locomotives were acquired and short passenger shuttles were operated.

Despite its short length, the CVR is home to three ex-Barry scrapyard main line steam locomotives under restoration. LNER locomotives have occasionally paid short visits.

Bo'ness & Kinneil Railway

The Scottish Railway Preservation Society took a long time to find a suitable length of line but built up a sizeable collection of locomotives and stock at its base in Falkirk. Two locomotives, NBR J36 0-6-0 No. 673 *Maude* and LNER D49 4-4-0 No. 246 *Morayshire,* saw main line railtour service in the 1980s. The SRPS eventually settled on the derelict remains of the branch to Bo'ness on the Firth of Forth nearby and moved lock, stock and barrel from Falkirk in 1980-81.

It was by then a greenfield site, the site of the original Bo'ness station, closed in 1956, by then occupied by a roundabout, but several historic buildings have been obtained and re-erected to provide a traditional railway setting. Bo'ness station opened in 1981, the line was extended to Kinneil in 1987 and to Birkhill in 1989. Since 2010 the passenger service has continued to Manuel on the Edinburgh-Glasgow main line and a new station has been constructed.

Until 2010, this section was used only for the movement of locomotives and stock and allowed the SRPS Railtours train to be based at Bo'ness since 1991, while SRPS steam locomotives and historic stock saw main line use in earlier years, notably running to the Shildon and Rainhill 150th anniversary celebrations in 1975 and 1980 respectively as well as railtours.

The railway is also the home of the Museum of Scottish Railways, which was opened in 1995 as the Scottish Railway Exhibition and extended in 2002.

Two steam centres were established at one-time GCR sites. The London Railway Preservation Society set up a large centre at Quainton Road station on the GC/Metropolitan line north of Aylesbury, which has become the Buckinghamshire Railway Centre. The Dinting Railway Centre based on the one-road shed near Glossop on the Woodhead route was a major player in main line railtour operations in the 1970s and 1980s but has closed; just the original shed now remains, in derelict condition. On the GER, a railway museum was established at North Woolwich, which was opened by the Queen Mother in 1984 but has now closed as the site is being redeveloped.

Three lengths of steam-worked railway have been built in LNER territory but on greenfield sites, at Mangapps Farm in Essex, Bressingham Gardens in Norfolk, and the North of England Open Air Museum at Beamish, County Durham. Another short length of line was the Lochty Private Railway on John Cameron's farm in Fife, Scotland, which was the trackbed of an NBR branch and was

BELOW: NER J72 0-6-0T No. 69023 at Layerthorpe on the last day of passenger services on the Derwent Valley Railway on September 2, 1979.

GER J15 0-6-0 No. 65462 at Castle Hedingham on the Colne Valley Railway on September 24, 2004.
GEOFF SILCOCK

briefly graced by A4 Pacific No. 60009 *Union of South Africa* until closure when the A4 resumed its main line career in 1973. Also in Scotland in more recent years, the Keith & Dufftown Railway has operated DMU services over 11 miles of a one-time GNSR route and the Royal Deeside Railway operates on Sundays over a one-mile section of the GNSR's Ballater branch which once carried Royal Trains en route to Balmoral.

In East Anglia, the Bure Valley and Wells & Walsingham railways are miniature lines laid on one-time GER trackbeds, while the South Tynedale Railway in Cumbria is a narrow gauge line running on part of the route of the NER's Alston branch towards Haltwhistle. The Middleton Railway in Leeds was never part of the LNER, being essentially an industrial line connecting with the Midland Railway, while the North Tyneside Railway with its associated Stephenson Railway Museum operates short-distance passenger services near Percy Main near Whitley Bay. A more recent development has seen the first trains operating over a short section of the Aln Valley Railway, near Alnwick in Northumberland.

The LNER's pioneer railway museum at York was replaced by a much grander National Railway Museum in 1975, converted from the NER locomotive shed north of York station and still recognisable as such with its two turntables. However, the structure was completely rebuilt and one of the two turntables removed so that this major part of 'preserved' one-time LNER infrastructure is no longer extant. The Head of Steam museum at Darlington was established in Darlington's one-time Stockton & Darlington Railway North Road station, and a new NRM outstation was built at Shildon, not in any sense 'preserved', but certainly in a historically significant location and close to Timothy

Hackworth's locomotive works and other surviving S&DR features.

While not a preserved heritage line, the North British Railway's 42-mile West Highland Extension from Fort William to Mallaig has carried a very successful steam-hauled service in summer since 1984.∎

BELOW: LNER D49 4-4-0 No. 246 *Morayshire* departs from Bo'ness station on the Bo'ness & Kinneil Railway.

CHAPTER 2

The National Collection

The LNER was one of the more enlightened Big Four companies in terms of locomotive preservation

LNER V2 2-6-2 No. 4771
***Green Arrow* passes Shipley on September 8, 1990.**

The beginnings of the National Collection can be traced back to NER days when such historically significant engines as the Stockton & Darlington's *Locomotion* and *Derwent* were acquired from industrial users for permanent preservation, partly stimulated by the S&D 50th anniversary in 1875.

The pre-Grouping railway companies set aside engines for preservation on a very piecemeal basis, such as the GNR's Stirling Single No. 1 in 1907. The Big Four companies after Grouping were also inconsistent, the GWR being particularly bad and the LMS, while it kept some engines, also cut some up after years of 'preservation'.

Best in this respect though was the LNER which inherited the NER's collection, and the GNR engine, and was obliged to stage an S&D 100th anniversary in 1925, also acted as a stimulus for the preservation of several more engines. More importantly, it directly led to the establishment of the railway museum at York, whose collection even expanded to include London Brighton & South Coast Railway 0-4-2 No. 214 *Gladstone* and Great Western record breaker No. 3440 *City of Truro*. NER engines in the museum from its opening were 0-6-0 No. 1275 and 2-4-0s Nos. 910 and 1463.

Further engines set aside by the LNER included the pioneer GNR Atlantic No. 990 *Henry Oakley*, much-rebuilt NER 2-2-4T No. 66 *Aerolite,* NER 4-4-0 No. 1621 and GNR large Atlantic No. 251. Other constituent companies did not fare so well although Gresley was known to favour saving a NBR Atlantic, and certainly an NER Pacific ought to have been saved.

BR set aside a number of engines in the 1950s, particularly the Scottish quartet, two of LNER origin. These; NBR 4-4-0 No. 256 *Glen Douglas* and GNSR 4-4-0 No. 49 *Gordon Highlander* were overhauled and put to work in 1959, restored to original livery. Then in 1960 came the publication of the British Transport Commission's list of engines to be 'officially' preserved.

In addition to those already preserved, additional LNER engines of pre-Grouping origin were the NER's T3 0-8-0 No. 901, the GCR's 8K 2-8-0 No. 102 and 11F 4-4-0 No. 506 *Butler-Henderson,* and the GER's T26 2-4-0 No. 490, S56 0-6-0T No. 87 and G58 0-6-0 No. 1217.

However the LNER's own illustrious history of locomotive building was to be represented by just Gresley's V2 2-6-2 No. 4771 *Green Arrow* and record-breaking streamlined A4 Pacific No. 4468 *Mallard,* Missing was a GER Claud Hamilton 4-4-0, *Flying Scotsman* or any other non-streamlined Gresley Pacific and any Thompson or Peppercorn Pacific. In fact we are fortunate that any non-streamlined LNER Pacific survived into preservation at all.

Only Nos. 506, 87, 490 and later No. 4468 found their way into the new Museum of British Transport, opened in Clapham in 1960, all of which had worked out of London. It was a long time before any others were put on public display although the Scottish engines retired to a museum in Glasgow in 1966.

Plans for museums at such places as Leicester and Doncaster came to nothing, and the 'other officially' preserved engines,

TOP: LNER A4 Pacific No. 4468 *Mallard* at York station on July 16, 1988.

LEFT: An LNER line-up at the Locomotion museum at Shildon in September 2010; N2 0-6-2T No. 1744, D49 4-4-0 No. 246 *Morayshire*, J72 0-6-0T No. 69023, A4 Pacific No. 4468 *Mallard* and V2 2-6-2 No. 4771 *Green Arrow.* DEE DAVISON

BELOW: NER 0-6-0 No. 1275 and NER Bo-Bo electric No. 1 in the National Railway Museum at York.

some immaculately restored, remained in store at Hellifield, Stratford or Preston Park. Only when the new National Railway Museum at York was opened were places found for everything.

By then of course private preservation had blossomed and some National Collection engines had already been placed on loan to heritage lines or societies, in some cases with plans for steaming.

No. 4771 *Green Arrow* went to Norwich where it was returned to steam, then Carnforth, before taking its place at the NRM. Again it was the Stockton & Darlington anniversary providing the impetus in 1975 just as it had in 1925.

GCR No. 506 *Butler-Henderson* went appropriately to the Great Central Railway at Loughborough where it was returned to steam. Other National Collection LNER locomotives steamed in preservation have been GNR 4-2-2 No. 1 and Atlantics Nos. 990 *Henry Oakley* and 251, GNSR 4-4-0 No. 49 *Gordon Highlander,* and NBR 4-4-0 No. 256 *Glen Douglas*, GCR 2-8-0 No. 63601, NER 0-8-0 No. 901, and LNER 2-6-2 No. 4771 *Green Arrow* and 4-6-2 No. 4468 *Mallard.*

The NRM's collection of LNER engines has expanded in more recent years with GNR J52 0-6-0ST No. 1247 being donated by its owner, and A3 Pacific No. 4472 *Flying Scotsman* finally joining the collection following purchase by the museum, giving a total of 22 LNER engines officially preserved, equalling the LMS total and more than from either of the other Big Four companies. ∎

CHAPTER 3

Preserved LNER steam locomotives

Privately preserved ex-LNER locomotives have contributed to a grand total of 53 now existing in preservation.

New-build LNER A1 Pacific No. 60163 _Tornado_ departs from Sheringham on the North Norfolk Railway in August 2012.

By the time of the Grouping in 1923, the LNER had inherited four historic preserved engines from the North Eastern Railway and one from the Great Northern Railway. The 1925 Stockton & Darlington centenary celebrations gave the newly-formed railway the incentive to add to this collection and led to the establishment of the railway museum at York.

By Nationalisation in 1945, the stock of preserved LNER steam engines had grown to 10, to which can be added Metropolitan 4-4-0T No. 23 at Neasden, although strictly never an LNER engine. BR added 10 more to the list of officially preserved engines.

In total, between 1959 and 1968, 23 LNER steam locomotives were purchased from BR for private preservation, two of which have since become part of the National Collection. Five were added from industrial service but only one from Barry scrapyard.

There are four new-build projects, two completed and one making good progress. A working replica of the S&D's _Locomotion No. 1_ headed the 1975 cavalcade at Shildon, LNER A1 Pacific No. 60163 _Tornado_ now proving what a capable design Peppercorn came up with, is the most high-profile, while the NER G5 0-4-4T is coming together at Shildon as funds permit, and after a slow start, it is hoped that one day a GER F5 2-4-2T will be seen again.

Without Barry scrapyard, the LNER would have come second in the league table of number of locomotives preserved from the Big Four companies, only the LMS beating it, partly by sheer size and partly as LMS engines were the last ones working on BR, with a dozen or so 'Black Fives' entering preservation at the end.

However, the LNER eventually came out last in the league table as only one made it to Barry scrapyard. Many early engines from the LNER constituents have been preserved but many have remained static exhibits in museums. Out of 52 locomotives of the LNER or its constituents' origin or design in total, 36 have been steamed in preservation since 1948, this compares with 65 out of 89 on the Southern for example.

Three GCR-designed 8K 2-8-0s remain in Australia, which would probably have become LNER O4s if they had returned to Britain. None has been restored but any attempt to repatriate one has so far failed.■

RIGHT: Stockton & Darlington 0-4-0 _Locomotion No. 1_ and 0-6-0 No. 25 _Derwent_ on display at Darlington Bank Top station in June 1972.

			BUILT	LNER CLASS	BR NUMBER	FIRST PRESERVED	CURRENT LOCATION
■ STOCKTON & DARLINGTON RAILWAY							
0-4-0		Locomotion No. 1	1825			Darlington	Darlington
0-6-0		25 Derwent	1845			Darlington	Darlington
■ NORTH EASTERN RAILWAY							
	2-2-4T	66 Aerolite	1851	X1		York	NRM York
1001	0-6-0	1275	1874			Darlington	NRM York
901	2-4-0	910	1875			Darlington	Kirkby Stephen
1463	2-4-0	1463	1885	E5		Darlington	Darlington
C	0-6-0	876	1889	J21	65033	Consett	Locomotion
H	0-4-0T	1310	1891	Y7		Middleton	Middleton
H	0-4-0T	985	1923	Y7	68088	Thurgarton	Beamish
M1	4-4-0	1621	1893	D17/1		York	Locomotion
T2	0-8-0	2238	1918	Q6	63395	Tyne Dock	NYMR
T3	0-8-0	901	1919	Q7	63460	Stratford	Darlington
P3	0-6-0	2392	1923	J27	65894	NCB Philadelphia	NYMR
E1	0-6-0T	69023 'Joem'	1951	J72	69023	KWVR	Wensleydale
■ GREAT NORTHERN RAILWAY							
	4-2-2	No. 1	1870			Doncaster	Locomotion
C1	4-4-2	990 Henry Oakley	1898	C2		York	Bressingham
J13	0-6-0ST	1247	1899	J52	68846	Marshmoor	Locomotion
C1	4-4-2	251	1902	C1		York	Barrow Hill
N2	0-6-2T	1744	1921	N2	69523	NCB Harworth	GCR
■ GREAT CENTRAL RAILWAY							
8K	2-8-0	102	1912	O4	63601	Stratford	GCR
11F	4-4-0	506 Butler-Henderson	1920	D11	62660	Clapham	Barrow Hill
■ GREAT EASTERN RAILWAY							
209	0-4-0ST	229	1876	Y5		Dean Forest	Flour Mill
T26	2-4-0	490	1894	E4	62785	Clapham	Bressingham
S56	0-6-0T	87	1904	J69	68633	Clapham	Bressingham
G58	0-6-0	1217	1905	J17	65567	Hellifield	Barrow Hill
X14	0-6-0	564	1912	J15	65462	Devons Road	NNR
L77	0-6-2T	999E	1924	N7	69621	Neville Hill	Churnet VR
■ GREAT NORTH OF SCOTLAND RAILWAY							
F	4-4-0	49 Gordon Highlander	1920	D40	62277	Dawsholm	Bo'ness
■ NORTH BRITISH RAILWAY							
G	0-4-0ST	42	1887	Y9	68095	Lytham	Bo'ness
C	0-6-0	673 Maude	1891	J36	65243	Falkirk	Bo'ness
K	4-4-0	256 Glen Douglas	1913	D34	62469	Dawsholm	Glasgow
■ METROPOLITAN RAILWAY							
	4-4-0T	23				Neasden	Covent Garden
E	0-4-4T	No. 1			L44 (LT)	Luton	Quainton Road
■ LONDON & NORTH EASTERN RAILWAY							
A3	4-6-2	4472 Flying Scotsman	1923		60103	Doncaster	NRM York
B12/3	4-6-0	8572	1928		61572	Devons Road	NNR
D49	4-4-0	246 Morayshire	1928		62712	Ardeer	Bo'ness
Y1	4wVBT	59	1933		Dep. 54	Middleton	Middleton
V2	2-6-2	4771 Green Arrow	1936		60800	Hellifield	Locomotion
A4	4-6-2	4488 Union of South Africa	1937		60009	Lochty	Thornton Jct
A4	4-6-2	4489 Dominion of Canada	1937		60010	Montreal	Montreal
A4	4-6-2	4498 Sir Nigel Gresley	1937		60007	Crewe	NYMR
A4	4-6-2	4496 Dwight D. Eisenhower	1937		60008	Green Bay USA	Green Bay USA
A4	4-6-2	4464 Bittern	1937		60019	York	Southall
A4	4-6-2	4468 Mallard	1938		60022	Clapham	NRM York
K4	2-6-0	3442 The Great Marquess	1938		61994	Neville Hill	Thornton Jct
J94	0-6-0ST	8077	1947		68077	KWVR	Sellindge
J94	0-6-0ST	8078	1947		68078	Southall	Southall
B1	4-6-0	1264	1947		61264	GCR	NYMR
B1	4-6-0	61306 Mayflower	1948		61306	Carnforth	NNR
A2	4-6-2	60532 Blue Peter	1948		60532	York	Barrow Hill
K1	2-6-0	62005	1949		62005	Neville Hill	NYMR
■ NEW BUILD							
	0-4-0	Locomotion No. 1	1975			Beamish	Beamish
A1	4-6-2	60163 Tornado	2008			Darlington	Darlington

CHAPTER 4

LNER Steam on the Main Line

In the preservation era, many former LNER steam engines have played a starring role, both on their home turf and in many cases, in territory far removed from the routes they were built for.

ABOVE: LNER V2 2-6-2 No. 4771 *Green Arrow* crosses Ais Gill viaduct with a southbound 'Cumbrian Mountain Express' on September 30, 1989.

Even disregarding the appearance of some particularly ancient machinery in steam at the S&D cavalcades of 1875 and 1925, the LNER has played a disproportionate role in the history of preserved steam on Britain's main lines.

The real beginning of active main line preserved steam was in 1938, when GNR Stirling Single No. 1 was brought out of retirement at York to help publicise the LNER's new streamlined expresses but also worked a couple of public excursions. This was followed after the Second World War and Nationalisation by two more GNR engines, Atlantics No. 990 *Henry Oakley* and No. 251, which came

LNER A3 Pacific No. 4472 *Flying Scotsman* picks up water from Danby Wiske water stops on its nonstop King's Cross-Edinburgh run on May 1, 1968, commemorating the 40th anniversary of the inauguration by the same locomotive of the first nonstop service between the two cities.
JOHN WHITELEY

out of York museum at Alan Pegler's instigation to work the 'Plant Centenarian' from King's Cross to Doncaster in 1953.

The first privately owned preserved steam engine to haul a passenger train on the main line was a fourth GNR engine, Captain Bill Smith's J52 0-6-0ST No. 1247 in 1959. Then came BR's Scottish quartet also in 1959, of which two were former LNER stock, GNSR 4-4-0 No. 49 *Gordon Highlander* and NBR 4-4-0 No. 256 *Glen Douglas,* which worked tours in Scotland until 1965.

A3 Pacific No. 4472 *Flying Scotsman* only just beat Lord Garnock's K4 mogul No. 3442 *The Great Marquess* in hauling a main line railtour in April 1963 but No. 4472 became the star, in the ownership of Alan Pegler who had actually masterminded the comeback of Nos. 990 and 251 a decade earlier. Nos. 4472 and 3442 were followed on to the main line by three more LNER engines before the October 1967 BR steam ban came into force, A4 Pacifics Nos. 4498 *Sir Nigel Gresley*, 60009 *Union of South Africa* and 60019 *Bittern*.

Up to that time, steam simply ran on main lines wherever it was practicable although the scope gradually reduced as watering and turning facilities disappeared. In fact King's Cross was a no-go area from 1964 to 1966. The BR ban on the operation of privately preserved steam engines from October 1967 did not apply to *Flying Scotsman* as Alan Pegler had a unique running agreement with BR, and so this LNER Pacific became the only steam engine able to run on any BR main line between August 1968 and August 1969, when it emigrated to America.

When steam returned to the main line in 1972 on a very limited basis after some experimental runs on the WR in 1971, the rules were very different. Only six routes were offered by BR initially, the LNER ones being Newcastle – Carlisle, and York –

GNR Stirling Single No. 1 heads an RCTS railtour from King's Cross to Peterborough, near St Neots, on September 11, 1938, the first enthusiasts' railtour to be hauled by a preserved steam locomotive. REG BATTEN

GNR Atlantics No. 990 *Henry Oakley* and No. 251 pass Werrington Junction with the 'Plant Centenarian' from King's Cross to Doncaster on September 20, 1953. BOB JOHNSON

Scarborough, A4 Pacific No. 4498 *Sir Nigel Gresley* leading the LNER main line steam revival by working on the former route in June 1972.

The first six routes were augmented the following year by Hull-Scarborough, Inverkeithing-Dundee, and later Edinburgh-Aberdeen and later included Newcastle-Middlesbrough, Leeds-Harrogate-York-Skipton, and Manningtree-March.

For the Rail 150 celebrations centred on Shildon, followed by the opening of the new National Railway Museum at York in 1975, BR gave one-off dispensation for that year only for a series of steam workings between Battersby and Whitby and more significantly from Sheffield to York and on to Newcastle over the ECML. From 1976 little changed but opening the routes from Sheffield to York and Leeds to York gave better operational flexibility particularly for inter-regional workings. While not an LNER route, the first steam train over the Settle & Carlisle line in 1978 was headed by the NRM's LNER V2 2-6-2 No. 4771 *Green Arrow*.

Apple green was very much to the fore from 1972 with No. 4771 *Green Arrow*, B1 No. 1306 *Mayflower*, K1 No. 2005 and D49 4-4-0 No. 246 *Morayshire* quickly seeing action. No. 4472 *Flying Scotsman* always seemed able to break many of the rules and for its 60th birthday in 1983, it was allowed to work three specials over the GN main line from Peterborough to York.

A one-time LNER route which saw a particularly welcome and ultimately long-lived and profitable return to steam was the West Highland extension from Fort William to Mallaig in 1984, with a regular five days per week operation throughout the summer ever since.

Apart from the brief visit by NBR 0-6-0 No. 673 *Maude* in 1984, LMS engines predominated until LNER K1 No. 2005 brought a touch of apple green to the Highlands in 1987.

The immortal A4 Pacific No. 4468 *Mallard* made a brief appearance on the main line in 1986-88, steam operations to Scarborough having been made possible once again by the reinstatement of its turntable.

East Anglia saw little main line steam for many years, the Manningtree-March route seeing just three trains powered by a Southern engine, but BR itself ran a series of shuttles between Bishops Stortford and Ely in 1991, shortly before Privatisation took place on April 1, 1994, and which really moved the goalposts for steam.

'The Elizabethan' in October that year saw nothing less than an A4 hauling a train out of King's Cross, the last steam departure from that terminus having been by *Flying Scotsman* in August 1969. Railtrack operated an 'open access' policy and was unable to impose the same rules on main line steam operation as BR had done. 'The Elizabethan' ran only to Peterborough, but it did not take long before A4s and others were running between King's Cross and York, Newcastle and even Edinburgh, despite overhead electrification of the route in 1988.

Two engines with somewhat chequered main line careers were the two Pacifics bought by Geoff Drury. While his A4, No. 60019 *Bittern*, made a number of runs in the 1960s and a couple more after the BR ban was lifted in the early 1970s, there was no sign of his A2, No. 60532 *Blue Peter* making a main line comeback and *Bittern* very quickly joined it in apparent exile.

It was the intervention of the North Eastern Locomotive Preservation Group that proved to be the A2's salvation, its long-awaited main line debut occurring in 1993. *Bittern* meanwhile went through two changes of ownership but when it did finally reappear in late 2007 it quickly proved itself the equal of the better-established streamliners.

As well as *Maude*, another 0-6-0 made it on to the main line; NER J27 0-6-0 No. 65894 making a couple of runs to Whitby with trains from the NYMR. This railway had been somewhat hesitant to extend its services to the popular resort just eight miles from its northern terminus at Grosmont but Privatisation made the sums now start to add up and after a few one-off workings on special occasions, trains began to run to Whitby on a regular basis. It has even proved possible for locomotives, stock and train crews to be certificated to different criteria to that which apply on high speed inter-city routes.

Similar rules have applied for running over London Transport routes, where locomotive owners have been allowed to crew their own locomotives under supervision.

GER-designed N7 0-6-2T No. 69621 saw some limited main line action in the early 1990s and the sole ex-Barry LNER engine, B1 4-6-0 No. 1264 returned to the main line in 1998. Finally Britain's only new-build main line engine to be completed so far is of LNER pedigree. A1 Pacific No. 60163 *Tornado* worked its first main line tour in January 2009 and rapidly established itself as Britain's most famous steam engine. ■

BELOW: On the groundbreaking run that proved that steam could run under 25kV overhead wires, LNER A4 Pacific No. 60009 *Union of South Africa* arrives at Peterborough with 'The Elizabethan' from King's Cross on October 30, 1994.

CHAPTER 5

Stockton & Darlington Railway

Much can still be seen of the world's first public railway, including two of its early engines, and a working replica of its very first steam engine, and the anniversary of its opening has been celebrated in style three times.

RIGHT: The spot where the first steam-hauled public passenger train commenced its journey from Shildon on September 27, 1825.

The Stockton and Darlington Railway was the world's first public passenger railway. There had been railways, particularly in north-east England for many years, and steam engines were in use on some but they were private lines serving mainly the coal industry. The S&DR was open to all, passenger and goods, but although much has been made of its pioneering use of steam traction, it was primarily worked by horses initially and passengers were subsidiary to its goods traffic.

Nevertheless it was to form the first section of what would nearly 100 years later become the London & North Eastern Railway, and this unique heritage was to shape not only the early development in railway preservation in this country but continue to influence the heritage railway industry right up to the present day.

Opened on September 27, 1825, between Witton Park in west Durham and Stockton-on-Tees via Darlington and connected to several collieries near Shildon, at 26 miles, it was the world's longest railway line at the time.

Over the next 38 years the S&DR steadily expanded into a substantial network serving south and west Durham, Cleveland and Westmorland. It was eventually taken over by the North Eastern Railway in 1863, but continued to operate independently for a further 10 years.

Darlington wool merchant Edward Pease had envisaged a horse-drawn plateway, but George Stephenson's steam engines were by then working on the Hetton colliery railway and Stephenson persuaded Pease to work his new line at least partly by steam.

The S&DR's track gauge was dictated by the horse-drawn wagons used in the older colliery waggonways but an additional half-inch was later added to reduce friction, as a result of which 4ft 8½in was subsequently adopted as standard gauge.

The first steam locomotive to run on the S&DR was 0-4-0 *Locomotion No 1*, built at Stephenson's works in Wylam and the opening day passenger train hauled by the locomotive took two

hours to complete the first 12 miles of the journey with most of the 600 passengers seated in open coal wagons. On its arrival at Stockton, the train was greeted by a crowd of 40,000 and a 21-gun salute.

The original regular passenger service though, consisted of a horse-drawn coach with horse provided by the driver. Steam traction was expensive in comparison with horse-drawn traffic, but it soon proved viable and economic. Steam engines could haul more wagons and haul them faster, so as steam technology became more reliable, horses were gradually abandoned and by 1833, it was entirely steam-operated.

Although at first, the S&DR simply owned the track and anyone could run trains on it, like Network Rail today, it proved a huge financial success and paved the way for modern rail

RIGHT: The replica S&DR 0-4-0 *Locomotion No. 1* leads the Rail 150 cavalcade from Shildon on August 31, 1975.

transport, with the railway adopting the procedures we now accept for railway operation.

William Bouch became the S&DR's locomotive engineer and in 1860, designed the first 4-4-0 to run in Britain.

The S&DR's expansion saw it grow to have a line crossing the Pennines to Tebay and Penrith in Cumberland. Some of the original S&DR is still in use today, particularly between Teesside, Darlington and Bishop Auckland but much closed with the contraction of the coal industry.

0-4-0 *Locomotion No. 1*

The Stockton & Darlington Railway's first steam locomotive, *Locomotion No. 1* was originally named *Active* and was built by George and Robert Stephenson's locomotive building company, Robert Stephenson and Co at Forth Banks, Newcastle in 1825. Four were built at a price of £600 each.

Locomotion built on Stephenson's pioneering steam locomotive which worked at Killingworth colliery. It used high-pressure steam from a centre-flue boiler, with a steam-blast in the chimney, to drive two vertical cylinders, enclosed inside the boiler. A pair of yokes above the cylinders transmitted the power downwards through connecting rods and it was one of the first locomotives to use coupling rods rather than chains or gears to link the driving wheels.

Delivered by road, *Locomotion No. 1* was first placed on rails at Heighington station and ran at speeds of around 12-15mph on the S&DR's opening train on September 27, 1825.

In 1828 its boiler exploded, killing the driver, but with steam engine design developing rapidly, *Locomotion* had become obsolete very quickly. It was later rebuilt and remained in service until 1841 when it was bought by Joseph Pease and Partners Ltd for use as a stationary pumping engine. On its eventual retirement from this duty in 1857, it was not scrapped but presented to the Stockton & Darlington Railway for permanent preservation and put on display in Alfred Kitching's workshop near Hopetown carriage works in Darlington until the 1880s, when it was placed on a pedestal in front of North Road station.

Locomotion No. 1 took pride of place under its own steam at the head of the NER's 1875 locomotive cavalcade celebrating the 50th anniversary of the opening of the S&DR. However, for the LNER's 100th anniversary event in 1925, while it still led the cavalcade from Darlington to Stockton complete with replica train, it was powered by a petrol engine in the tender, an early example of 'modern' traction. In 1892 it was put on show along with the S&DR 0-6-0 *Derwent* on one of the platforms at Darlington's Bank Top station on the East Coast Main Line. Becoming part of the National Collection, the locomotive was removed from its plinth in 1975, exactly 150 years after its debut on the S&DR, and is now on display at the Head of Steam museum at Darlington's one-time S&DR North Road station.

For the 1975 150th anniversary S&DR cavalcade from Shildon, a working replica of *Locomotion No. 1* was built, by a team led by

engineer Michael Satow, and after leading the cavalcade, the engine has been in regular service at the Beamish Museum in County Durham.

0-6-0 No. 25 *Derwent*

Derwent was designed by Timothy Hackworth and built in 1845 by William and Alfred Kitching for the Stockton and Darlington Railway. It is typical of earlier Kitching designs, with outside cylinders to the rear of the boiler.

On withdrawal from service in 1869, it was sold to Pease & Partners for use on their colliery lines and spent some time at the construction of the Waskerley Reservoir in Co. Durham. It took part in the Stephenson Centenary celebrations at Newcastle in 1881 and Queen Victoria's Diamond Jubilee in 1887.

Like many early locomotives which found a new lease of life in industrial service, its owners recognised its historical importance and *Derwent* was presented to the North Eastern Railway in 1898 for preservation. After restoration, it ran under its own steam in the 1925 S&DR centenary cavalcade, achieving 12mph. Apart from this outing, it was on display until 1975 alongside *Locomotion No. 1* on a plinth on one of the platforms at Darlington Bank Top station.

It was removed in 1975 and restored to near original condition, and put on display in the Head of Steam museum at Darlington North Road. ∎

ABOVE: S&DR 0-6-0 No. 25 *Derwent* being steam tested before its appearance in the LNER's 1925 S&DR centenary cavalcade. RAILWAY MAGAZINE

S&DR 0-6-0 No. 25 *Derwent* on display in the Head of Steam museum at Darlington. ROBIN JONES

Locomotion No. 1 on display in the Head of Steam museum at North Road station in Darlington. ROBIN JONES

CHAPTER 6

North Eastern Railway

Once merged with the Stockton & Darlington Railway, the NER inherited the world's first public railway and so made a significant contribution to the early days of steam preservation.

The North Eastern Railway was created in 1854, when four existing companies were combined. The first two were the York Newcastle & Berwick Railway, which formed most of the NER's portion of the ECML and George Hudson's York & North Midlands Railway, again self-explanatory, but it also included Stephenson's Whitby & Pickering Railway.

These were joined by the Leeds Northern Railway, running via Harrogate and Ripon to Thirsk, and the Malton & Driffield Railway.

Unlike many other pre-Grouping companies, the NER had a near monopoly of its territory, which stretched from Doncaster to Berwick, and to the east, plus lines as far west as Carlisle. The NER's main line formed the middle link of what became the East Coast Main Line from King's Cross to Edinburgh, between the Great Northern Railway and the North British Railway.

The ECML was not completed until as late as 1871 when the line from Shaftholme Junction to Selby was built to avoid trains travelling over the Lancashire & Yorkshire via Knottingley to reach York.

The company also took over the Stockton & Darlington Railway in 1863. Its headquarters were at York while it also inherited locomotive and carriage works at Darlington, Gateshead, York, Shildon and elsewhere.

The NER inherited the country's first station with a classic curved steel overall roof, Newcastle Central, from the York Newcastle & Berwick Railway, and the NER was to build probably the most impressive set of principal stations of any British railway company, the four largest, at Newcastle, Darlington, York and Hull all still surviving.

The NER is well represented in preservation mainly by the North Yorkshire Moors Railway, but various other stretches of NER line or its former constituents are also preserved including the Tanfield, Wensleydale, Weardale and Eden Valley railways.

The first locomotive superintendent on the NER, from 1854, was Edward Fletcher, who came from the York Newcastle & Berwick Railway. Like many engineers at the time, he designed engines on a largely one-off basis and there was very little standardisation. Fortunately, one of Fletcher's locomotives has survived, the successful express 2-4-0 No. 910.

Alexander McDonnell who came from the Great Southern and Western Railway of Ireland in 1883, was unpopular with the drivers and was quickly forced to resign. There was then an interval during which the job was covered by a locomotive committee chaired by Henry Tennant. Remarkably, one of Tennant's locomotive committee engines has survived, 2-4-0 No. 1463, largely by virtue of its being one of the last survivors just as the 1925 S&D centenary celebrations were under way.

The NER was brought into the modern age by the Worsdell brothers. Thomas Worsdell, from 1885, was one of Britain's greatest advocates of compounding and many of his designs used the two-cylinder system of August von Borries, usually in conjunction with simple-expansion versions of the same engines for comparison.

Most of the compounds were rebuilt as simples by his brother and successor Wilson Worsdell who took over in 1890.

Wilson introduced the system of class designations, starting with 'A' for the first, and adding a number for later developments of each. This system was reorganised somewhat in 1914 and was eventually combined with the similar but less refined GNR system to produce the LNER classification system.

Thomas Worsdell's designs are only represented in preservation by a couple of H class 0-4-0Ts but Wilson Worsdell introduced some classes which have become well-known in view of their longevity and we still have examples of his C and P3 (J21 and J27) 0-6-0s, the M1 4-4-0 No. 1621 and the J72 0-6-0T which was still being built by BR in the 1950s. Another Worsdell product, the G5 0-4-4T, is in the process of being recreated in a new-build project in the North East.

Sir Vincent Litchfield Raven KBE (1859-1934) was the last chief mechanical engineer of the NER from 1910 to Grouping in 1923. He began his career with the NER as a pupil of Edward Fletcher. By 1893 he was assistant to Wilson Worsdell who was then the locomotive superintendent. In this post he was involved for the first

time with an electrification project, as the NER was electrifying the North Tyneside suburban route in 1904.

He became chief mechanical engineer on Wilson Worsdell's retirement in 1910, the title of the post having changed in 1902. Raven developed some of Worsdell's designs, such as the T2 0-8-0, as well as introducing designs of his own. In particular he favoured a three-cylinder design, driving on the leading coupled axle. This was applied to a series of locomotives, culminating in the NER A2 Pacific for express passenger work. Generally considered more successful were the class Z Atlantics, which had a good reputation on ECML expresses.

Raven was a great enthusiast of electrification, and in 1915, the line from Shildon in the south-west Durham coalfield and Newport, on Teesside, was electrified at 1500v DC overhead in order to improve the performance of coal trains from Shildon to Middlesbrough. Ten centre-cab 1100hp electric locomotives were built at Darlington.

Following the success of the Shildon-Newport scheme, Raven was keen to see the electrification of the main line from York to Newcastle, also at 1500v DC. but the Grouping led to the plans not proceeding further and it was not taken any further by the LNER.

The Grouping in 1923 saw Nigel Gresley of the Great Northern Railway selected as the LNER's chief mechanical engineer and Raven briefly became a technical adviser, before resigning in 1924.

Sadly, none of Raven's express or passenger designs survived and his work is today represented by two long-lived freight designs, the T2 and T3 (Q6 and Q7) 0-8-0s. It is particularly unfortunate that none of his A2 Pacifics survived but they were quickly ousted by Gresley's products after Grouping. The B16 4-6-0s, which were built in considerable quantities, and were a familiar sight across the NER system until well into the 1960s were also all scrapped.

NER P3 0-6-0 No. 2392 climbs the 1-in-49 past Darnholm on the one-time NER North Yorkshire Moors Railway on January 13, 1991.

ABOVE: NER 2-2-4T No. 66
Aerolite in the National
Railway Museum at York.

ABOVE RIGHT: NER 2-4-0
No. 910 is towed past
Heighington by LNER A3
Pacific No. 4472 *Flying
Scotsman* in the Rail 150
cavalcade from Shildon on
August 31, 1975.

BOTTOM RIGHT: NER 2-4-0
No. 1463 on display in the
Head of Steam museum,
Darlington.

BELOW: NER 0-6-0 No. 1275
in the National Railway
Museum at York.

2-2-4T No. 66 *Aerolite*

No. 66 *Aerolite* was built in 1869 as a replacement for an engine of
the same name built by Kitsons for the Great Exhibition in 1851,
which was destroyed in a collision in 1868. The engine, like its
predecessor, was used to haul the mechanical engineer's saloon.
Originally a 2-2-2 well tank, side tanks were added in 1886, and
around this time it received the number 66.

In 1892 *Aerolite* was rebuilt into a 4-2-2, destroying much of
the original engine. The well tank was removed, larger side tanks
fitted, and the two-cylinder Worsdell-von Borries compounding
system applied. In 1902 it was again rebuilt, into a 2-2-4T.

Being completely non-standard and with a unique wheel
arrangement, it was classified X1 by the LNER, but continued in
service doing the job it was originally designed for until it was
withdrawn in 1933 and preserved in 1934 at the LNER's York
museum. It is now a static exhibit at the NRM but cannot be
considered representative of any particular design era or type.

1001 class 0-6-0 No. 1275

The 'long boiler' dates to a Stephenson design of 1842, at a time
when there was a controversy about keeping the centre of gravity
low, and the long boiler with six coupled wheels continued for
slow, heavy, freight work. A total of 192 1001 class 0-6-0s were
built from 1852 by a number of private manufacturers, as well as
the NER's own works at Darlington and Shildon.

The small size of the firebox might have seemed unusual in
later years, but was ideal when trains often spent long periods
standing, waiting for a path, or when shunting. A minimum
amount of fuel would have delivered sufficient heat to the large
boiler to start heavy loads.

The last 10 NER 1001s went into service in 1875 and many
were rebuilt in the following 25 years. The last was withdrawn
in 1923.

Having travelled an official total of 908,984 miles No. 1275
featured in the 1925 S&DR centenary cavalcade and was
preserved at the LNER's new York museum, later taking its place
at the new NRM in York in 1975.

901 class 2-4-0 No. 910

Between 1872 and 1882, 55 of Edward Fletcher's 901 class 2-4-0s
were built for the NER.

From their introduction they put in excellent service on the
Newcastle-Edinburgh and Newcastle-York runs hauling 160 to
170-ton loads.

Twenty-nine of the class were withdrawn between 1913 and
1914 but the First World War led to a shortage of motive power
and new work was found for them, some on the line between
Scarborough and Bridlington but the majority working from
Darlington on passenger services over the former Stockton &
Darlington Stainmore route to Kirkby Stephen, Penrith and Tebay.
By 1923 only 10 of the class remained and the now preserved
No. 910 was among the final five to be withdrawn from service.

It was retained by the NER and put on display in the museum
at York. It is currently on display in one-time home territory at
Kirkby Stephen East.

1463 class 2-4-0 No. 1463

When McDonnell suddenly resigned from his position of
locomotive superintendent of the NER in September 1884, seven
of the 38 class 4-4-0s had been delivered, but they were no

improvement on the old Fletcher 901 class 2-4-0s they were meant to supersede.

So, when a successor to McDonnell could not immediately be appointed, and the NER urgently needed a new express locomotive, the NER's general manager, Henry Tennant, chaired a special committee to quickly design an express locomotive, the first one entering service in May 1885, known as the 1463 class but nicknamed 'Tennants'.

Obviously direct descendents of Fletcher's 901s, 20 were built in 1885, 10 each by Darlington and Gateshead works.

Worsdell-pattern boilers were fitted between 1892 and 1896 as the original boilers wore out unusually quickly, but nevertheless the engines proved very successful, although relegated to more secondary duties by the LNER after Grouping when they were reclassified as E5.

Withdrawals started in 1926, and the last to go was No. 1474 from York in February 1929. The first of the class, No. 1463 was retained by the LNER and put on display in York's museum in 1927.

C class 0-6-0 No. 65033

When appointed by the NER, T W Worsdell found an urgent need for new goods engines, the newest being McDonnell's 59 class 0-6-0s., and none of his engines had ever proved satisfactory. Worsdell had come from the GER where one of his successful designs had been the Y14 0-6-0. He enlarged the design to produce the NER C class and after the first three simple engines, 171 were built as compounds, as favoured by Worsdell.

Worsdell reported that the compound locomotives were much more economical than the simple ones but he retired in 1890 and was succeeded by his brother Wilson Worsdell, who did not share the same enthusiasm for compounding, so Wilson had the last two batches built as simples, classified C1.

The NER decided to convert all compounds to simple in 1894 and after priority had been given to the passenger locomotives, the last C class compound was rebuilt in 1913 and the whole class became 'C'.

Gateshead built the majority of the 201 engines but 30 were built at Darlington. The LNER designated them J21.

The transfer of six GER E4 2-4-0s to work over the Stainmore route in the 1930s resulted in eight J21s being loaned to the GE section. Modifications were needed to make them fit the GE loading gauge, including new chimneys but by the time the redesigning was done, the J21s were back in the North East. However, as it was still thought that the J21s might have to work on the GE during the war, all the engines were modified anyway.

Although originally designed for goods traffic and mostly not fitted for continuous braking, the LNER increasingly used them on passenger trains including the Newcastle-South Shields line, and most were eventually fitted with appropriate braking systems.

The C class was one of the NER's most numerous classes and at Grouping, comprised no less than 10% of the railway's locomotive stock, 205 remaining in service for 34 years. They were displaced to secondary lines as larger engines were introduced and many moved away from the North East, but they became increasingly associated with the one-time Stockton & Darlington Stainmore route across the Pennines.

NER C class 0-6-0 No. 876 in action at Beamish. BEAMISH

Fifty one years after NER J21 0-6-0 No. 65033 steamed through Kirkby Stephen East on May 7, 1960, the engine returned for the Stainmore 150 event in August 2011. MAURICE BURNS

ABOVE: NER H class 0-4-0T No. 1310 heads a goods train on the Balm Road branch on the Middleton Railway in Leeds.

No. 1310 departs from East Tanfield with a short coal train on September 8, 2012.
HENRY ELLIOTT

Withdrawal of the class started as long ago as 1929 but the last ones would survive another 33 years. Seventy-seven entered BR service in 1948 but by 1959, only five members of the class survived, based at South Blyth, Tyne Dock and Tweedmouth. The last to be withdrawn was No. 65033 in April 1962.

This engine, NER No. 876, was built in March 1889 as a compound and rebuilt as a simple in December 1908. In 1939, as LNER J21 No. 5033, it was withdrawn, but was reinstated after the wartime motive power shortage and allocated to Hull Dairycoates. When last overhauled at Darlington in August/September 1956, it had been fitted with an unsuperheated boiler with the distinctive shorter smokebox. In August 1958, allocated to South Blyth for the third time in its career, it had a complete repaint on May 5, 1960 in preparation for the RCTS and Stockton & Darlington Locomotive Society 'J21 Railtour' two days later. After a short spell at Heaton, No. 65033 returned to South Blyth for the fourth time and continued to work for just over a year before withdrawal on April 23, 1962.

No. 65033 had become something of a 'celebrity' engine having worked the 'J21 Railtour', which was the last J21 working over the Stainmore route. The route was from Darlington to Tebay, over Shap to Carlisle and back to Darlington via Penrith, Kirkby Stephen East, West Auckland and the Shildon curve.

No. 65033 was reserved for the National Collection, but this decision was reviewed as it was no longer in original condition, having been built as a compound. However, this did result in the engine being put to one side at Darlington and not scrapped. While official preservation was still on the cards, No. 65033 was in the company of No. 65099 which was withdrawn on October 20, 1961, with cracked frames and it seems likely that No. 65033 received the boiler from No. 65099.

It stood for no less than five years until being saved at the eleventh hour in June 1968, four days before being removed for scrap, by Dr Frank Atkinson CBE, the founder of Beamish, the North of England Open Air Museum, which was very much in its infancy at the time.

No. 65033 was quickly moved to the locomotive shed at Consett steelworks on June 7, 1968, and, in 1970, transferred to the Tanfield Railway where restoration work was undertaken allowing a return to steam as No. 876 in NER green. In 1975 the engine arrived at its new permanent home at Beamish and worked occasionally but with the expiry of the boiler certificate in December 1983, it retired and was stored in the open until 1999.

It is surprising how much a steam engine can deteriorate while in open storage for many years, and although steamable until 1976, by 2009 the engine appeared to be almost beyond economic repair.

Nevertheless The Locomotive Conservation & Learning Trust was set up by North Norfolk Railway director Julian Birley and No. 876 was moved from Beamish to Bill Parker's Flour Mill workshops in the Forest of Dean for an initial inspection to establish the work required to return it to working order.

It was then transferred to the North Norfolk Railway, but no progress was made and in May 2010, No. 876 was moved to the Locomotion museum at Shildon, and cosmetically restored as No. 65033. It is still intended that it will be returned to working order in a joint project with the National Railway Museum, and an application to the Heritage Lottery Fund is in preparation.

LEFT: The two surviving NER H class 0-4-0Ts, Nos. 1310 and 985 head a train of NER coaches at Beamish in September 2012.
ROBIN PATRICK

BELOW: Soon after returning to steam, NER Y7 0-4-0T No. 68088 is seen at Loughborough on the Great Central Railway on May 26, 1986.

BOTTOM: No. 68088 has been well travelled since its return to steam and is seen on a Sentimental Journeys' photo charter in Boston docks in 2000. ROBIN JONES

H class 0-4-0T

Designed by T W Worsdell, six H class 0-4-0Ts were built in 1888. Their simple, basic design was well suited to the tight curves and poor-quality track which they ran on. The H proved so successful that the NER ordered a further 10 in 1891, and three more in 1897. Another five were ordered by the LNER in 1923.

Their small size meant these engines did not have a bunker in the traditional position behind the cab, so coal was piled up on top of the side tanks immediately in front of the cab.

They were originally fitted with dumb buffers, but these were changed for small round buffers during the 1930s, some also gaining vacuum brakes during this period.

Dock work was hit hard by the depression, and between 1929 and 1932 the 16 locomotives which made up the first two batches delivered were withdrawn, nine being sold to industrial use while the remainder were scrapped.

0-4-0T No. 1310

NER H class No. 1310, built at Gateshead in 1891, was one of the first batches of the class built and was an early withdrawal by the LNER in 1931.

It was sold to Robert Frazer & Sons, and sold on to Pelaw Main Collieries Ltd in 1933. It passed to the National Coal Board in 1948, which renumbered it 63. With the closure of much of the Pelaw Main system in 1959, the engine was sent to the nearby Bowes Railway where it worked at Ravensworth Ann Colliery but was quickly transferred again to Watergate Colliery on the Tanfield branch.

On withdrawal in 1965, it was bought by the Steam Power Trust, and has been preserved at the Middleton Railway since June 16, 1965.

An overhaul at Middleton was completed in 2011 and the engine entered service again after nine years out of traffic.

0-4-0T No. 985

One of the last batch of the class, No. 985 was completed by the LNER at Darlington in 1923, and was renumbered 8088 in 1946. The class was designed for duties on Tyneside, at Hull docks, and within Darlington works, but No. 8088 is known to have worked at Stratford works between 1943 and 1952.

One of only two to make it to Nationalisation, it became BR No. 68088 but was transferred to departmental stock. It was sold to the National Coal Board in November 1952 and worked at Bentinck and Thurgarton collieries in Nottinghamshire until 1964 when it was purchased by the Y7 Preservation Society. Stored for many years at Thurgarton, it moved to the Great Central Railway at Loughborough in 1981 where it was returned to steam in 1983.

From 2004, the engine was based on the North Norfolk Railway, where it was overhauled at Weybourne but in December 2010 it was agreed that when its overhaul was completed, No. 985 would be based at Beamish Museum for three years.

NER M1 4-4-0 No. 1621 outside the Locomotion museum at Shildon.

M1 4-4-0 No. 1621

The M1 class 4-4-0 was Wilson Worsdell's first express passenger locomotive for the NER. In 1892, he had initially proposed a locomotive similar to his brother's F class with a smaller boiler, Stephenson valve gear, and simple expansion.

The exact proposal was not accepted, but the NER decided that one compound and 20 simple expansion express locomotives should be built. The compound locomotive was initially classed as M, and the 20 M1s were built at Gateshead between 1892 and 1894.

The later Q class was very similar to the M1 and both were built to haul expresses on the ECML, initially allocated to St Margaret's, Newcastle, and York and put to work on the York to Edinburgh leg of the newly introduced 2.30pm dining trains. The locomotives were heavily used during the 1895 'Race to the North' and in the final week of the races, the train was reduced from 120 to 105 tons and the M1s were used singly.

On the final night, York to Newcastle was covered in 78.5 minutes at an average speed of 61.6mph, while Newcastle to Edinburgh was reached in 113 minutes at an average of 66mph, liberties possibly having been taken with some speed restrictions.

The compound M was reclassified and the M1s became Ms. Unlike the Ms, most of the Qs received superheaters at the same time as piston valves and generally displaced the Ms from the top jobs, but the new D20 4-4-0s soon displaced both. Between 1910 and 1918, the Atlantics were introduced, relegating all of the NER's 4-4-0s to lesser duties.

Although the NER classed the M and Q as different classes, they were very similar locomotives once fitted with piston valves. The LNER combined the Ms and Qs into Class D17; M becoming D17/1 and Q becoming D17/2. At the Grouping, they were allocated to various NER sheds for secondary passenger services, and three were even loaned to the GE area in 1927.

Normal withdrawals of D17s started in 1931, but two D17/1s and seven D17/2s survived to the outbreak of the Second World War. The former were withdrawn in 1945, and No. 1621 was restored to NER condition and placed in the LNER's York museum. The last two D17/2s just survived into BR days but were withdrawn on February 7, 1948.

T2 0-8-0 No. 2238

Wilson Worsdell's T1 0-8-0s met the initial increases in the NER's mineral traffic at the turn of the century, but a large upsurge in traffic meant that more locomotive power was required. Raven designed his T2 class based on the T1 with a larger boiler. A total of 120 T2s were built between 1913 and 1921 in six batches.

The T2s were an unqualified success. By combining Worsdell's motion with the B15 boiler and the Schmidt superheater, Raven managed to create a strong and reliable locomotive which gave good service right up to the end of BR steam. They required very few modifications during their lives, although from 1930 the engines, reclassified Q6 by the LNER, had their Schmidt superheaters replaced with Robinson ones to bring them in line with LNER practice, and the boiler was redesigned in 1938.

The T2s were initially allocated to sheds in the North East for coal traffic, but by 1920 they would occasionally be used for medium- and long-distance freight as well. During LNER ownership, the Q6s

BELOW: NER Q6 0-8-0 No. 3395 on a members' special near Goathland on the North Yorkshire Moors Railway in August 1971.
MAURICE BURNS

Restored to NER livery as No. 2238, the T2 0-8-0 departs from Levisham on the North Yorkshire Moors Railway on October 31, 1976.

NER Q6 0-8-0 No. 63395 heads a goods train south through Newtondale on the North Yorkshire Moors Railway in November 2007.

NER Q6 0-8-0 No. 63395 at Woodthorpe Lane on the Great Central Railway in February 2009.
PHIL WATERFIELD

BELOW: NER Q7 0-8-0 No. 901 passes Water Ark on the North Yorkshire Moors Railway in September1994 .

tended to venture further afield including trips to Manchester via the Woodhead Tunnel, and after 1930 they were seen north of the Tyne. In the 1940s they also ventured south to Peterborough and March.

Withdrawals started in 1963, and the last Q6 was withdrawn in September 1967, at the very end of BR steam in the North East.

The North Eastern Locomotive Preservation Group was originally founded to raise money to secure an NER J27 0-6-0 for preservation but it decided to be a little more ambitious and go for a Q6 as well. One of the last working Q6s, No. 63395 was the engine selected and although it was a close-run thing, sufficient money was raised to secure an example of both classes at the end of steam in the North East in September 1967.

The Q6 was initially housed in the locomotive shed at Tyne Dock where restoration commenced but it was moved to Hartlepool on September 4, 1968, then to the roundhouse at Thornaby in February 1969, where it was first steamed in the group's ownership in October 1969.

The locomotive was moved to the North Yorkshire Moors Railway on May 26, 1970, becoming the first main line locomotive to be based on the line. In LNER livery as No. 3395, it starred in most of the early members' open days hauling short-distance shuttle trains from Goathland but was withdrawn for a full overhaul.

This was completed in the summer of 1975 and when the engine emerged immaculate in fully lined-out NER black livery, carrying the number 2238, it was arguably the finest volunteer restoration job carried out on a steam locomotive to date. No. 2238 was certified to run over BR metals to take part in the Stockton & Darlington 150th anniversary cavalcade at Shildon, returning to Grosmont from Darlington immediately afterwards.

The NYMR was now open for business and the Q6 saw regular use for a number of years. A more protracted overhaul completed in 2007 saw it revert to its BR identity of No. 63395 making it popular for goods train photo charters and it made working visits to other heritage lines including the Great Central Railway. It remains in regular use on NYMR passenger services but its long wheelbase makes it less than ideal for such work on a sharply curving route.

T3 0-8-0 No. 901

Although Raven's T2 0-8-0 was proving to be very successful, the NER approved a three-cylinder 0-8-0 design to be built in 1919 as class T3, based on the great success being enjoyed by Raven's other three-cylinder designs. NER practice was to initially build 10 of a new locomotive type, however, only five Q7s were built in 1919, suggesting there was no real need for the engines.

A month after the first of the T3s, No. 901 was outshopped from Darlington in November 1919, the NER organised a test train, over the Newcastle to Carlisle line, including the company's dynamometer car to record the locomotive's performance. With 1402 tons in tow, there were no problems starting on a 1-in-298 gradient and with a reduced load of 787 tons, the engine coped comfortably with gradients as severe as 1-in-107.

Ten more T3s were built by the LNER in 1924, even though the company was busy reconditioning ex-ROD GCR-designed O4 2-8-0s for less than half the price.

Now classified Q7, of the new engines two were allocated to York and four to Hull, where they worked on level track where the trains they were able to haul were far longer than the loops and sidings which had to accommodate them.

The remaining four went to Tyne Dock where eventually all 15 were allocated, and where they performed the duties they were designed for, hauling 700-ton trains of iron-ore hoppers to the steelworks at Consett 1000ft above sea level on gradients as steep as 1-in-35 in top-and-tail fashion. This they did successfully until the arrival of BR Standard 9F 2-10-0s in the 1950s. BR retired all 15 of the Q7s in late 1962.

Surprisingly, and reflecting the mystery as to why the Q7s were built in the first place, the Q7 was selected for inclusion in the BTC list of engines for 'official' preservation. While it was entirely appropriate that a Raven three-cylindered engine should be included, the far more numerous B16 4-6-0 which also survived into the 1960s might appear a more obvious choice and the Q7 was not chosen simply to represent the 0-8-0 as an LNWR Super D was also included.

Nevertheless after a period of storage at Darlington works, No. 63460 joined the collection being assembled at Stratford

NER Q7 0-8-0 No. 901 in the Head of Steam museum at Darlington.

works in October 1964, unusually moving to the other store at Hellifield in December 1967 and then to Preston Park on August 24, 1968.

Following the opening of the National Railway Museum in 1975, the relics stored at Preston Park were all moved out in November 1977 either to the NRM or on loan to other centres. The Q7 went initially to the NRM but was then placed on loan to the North Eastern Locomotive Preservation Group, an organisation with a proven track record of locomotive restoration. The engine was hauled by preserved Brush type 2 diesel D5500 to Grosmont on the NYMR on April 7, 1978.

Nevertheless it was September 1990 before the Q7 was returned to steam spending a number of years in regular NYMR passenger service, running in LNER livery as No. 901.

On expiry of its boiler certificate it was agreed that No. 901 should become a static exhibit, spending periods at the NRM, the Locomotion museum at Shildon and the Head of Steam museum at Darlington.

NER J27 0-6-0 No. 65894 heads a goods train up the climb to Kelling Heath on the North Norfolk Railway on September 4, 1997.

P3 0-6-0 No. 2392

The NER P3 0-6-0 was designed by Wilson Worsdell and was a relatively minor modification of the existing P2. Initially 80 were built between 1906 and 1909 in five batches by the NER's Darlington works, North British, Beyer Peacock, and Robert Stephenson.

Twelve years later, a batch of 25 J27s were built at Darlington with Schmidt superheaters and piston valves, which were delivered in 1921-22 and were followed by a final order of 10 made in December 1922 and built by the LNER at Darlington. Classified J27 by the LNER, the superheated J27s could be identified by their extended smokeboxes.

After the Second World War, the J27s were concentrated on hauling heavy mineral trains. Withdrawals began in March 1959, but by June 1966, 36 were still putting in hard work hauling coal in County Durham and South Northumberland. The last ones were withdrawn from the Blyth area where they operated the short trip workings between the nearby coalfield and shipping staithes, finally finishing in September 1967.

One, BR No. 65894, was purchased directly from BR by the North Eastern Locomotive Preservation Group on December 1, 1967, after a long, hard, fundraising campaign. Stored initially at Tyne Dock, some restoration commenced but it was restored to working order at the then still functioning National Coal Board workshops at Philadelphia, Co. Durham, first being steamed in December 1968.

Despite BR's steam ban, the J27 moved under its own steam from Philadelphia via Newcastle Central station to Thornaby shed on April 11, 1969, where restoration work continued, but the final touches, including the fitting of vacuum brake and steam heating apparatus for working passenger trains, were by the group's volunteers at ICI Billingham.

The immaculate P3 in NER lined black livery moved to the North Yorkshire Moors Railway on October 23, 1971, where it entered service the following weekend hauling members' trains and continued to work on occasional open days. It was selected to haul the NYMR's official reopening train conveying the Duchess of Kent in 1973 and was only prevented from running on the main line to Whitby by industrial action.

It has been a well-travelled engine in preservation, taking part in the Rail 150 S&DR cavalcade at Shildon, visiting heritage lines including the North Norfolk, Nene Valley and East Lancashire railways, and even heading a couple of Pullman dining trains between Grosmont and Whitby.

It spent the period from 1977 to 1982 on display in the National Railway Museum and had a further overhaul by NELPG members at ICI Wilton, returning to the NYMR in May 1996 in BR livery as No. 65894. For the last five years of its boiler certificate, it reverted to NER livery and is now under overhaul in Darlington, the work again being carried out by NELPG volunteers.

With four LNER Gresley teak coaches in tow, NER P3 0-6-0 No. 2392 departs from Goathland on the North Yorkshire Moors Railway in October 2002.

LEFT: NER P3 0-6-0 No. 2392 heads a short goods train near Levisham on the North Yorkshire Moors Railway on October 11, 1987.

NER J72 0-6-0T No. 69023 *Joem* on early Santa special duties at Oakworth on the Keighley & Worth Valley Railway in December 1968. MAURICE BURNS

On its first day in service in 1988, *Joem* departs from Embsay, on what was then known as the Yorkshire Dales Railway. MAURICE BURNS

J72 0-6-0T No. 69023

The NER E1 0-6-0T was designed by Wilson Worsdell for shunting, with inside cylinders and Stephenson valve gear. It was a development of the earlier E class designed by T W Worsdell.

A total of 113 locomotives were built: 50 by the NER, 25 for the NER by Armstrong Whitworth & Co and unusually, in 1925, another 10 by the LNER at the former GNR Doncaster works. But this was not the end of the story and, classified J72 by the LNER, this is a rare example of a class which was built, substantially unchanged, under pre-Grouping, post-Grouping and BR administrations, with another 28 being built by BR in 1949-1951.

Towards the end of steam, a couple of BR-built J72s were transferred into departmental stock and Departmental Locomotive No. 59 was purchased by Ronald Ainsworth and moved to the Keighley & Worth Valley Railway under its own steam via Newcastle, York and Leeds in mid-October 1967, where it worked in NER green livery, carrying the name *Joem*, after the owner's parents Joseph and Emily. It hauled trains during the first years of KWVR operation and featured, hauling the Old Gentleman's Saloon, in the 1970 film The Railway Children.

However, it was moved away from the KWVR to nearby Embsay in 1975 on what was known as the Yorkshire Dales Railway at the time, but it was only occasionally used here. Eventually it was purchased by the Derwent Valley Railway, a private line east of York which still handled freight traffic and launched a regular steam passenger operation, to complement the nearby National Railway Museum.

Arriving on February 5, 1977, the engine worked for a couple of summer seasons, but it was not a success and as freight traffic dwindled the line closed and *Joem* went on display in the NRM in January 1981.

A return to active service beckoned when it was purchased by NELPG and it moved to the NYMR for restoration on January 4, 1983. Since its return to steam it was deemed too small for

The Wilson Worsdell-designed NER J72 0-6-0T No. 69023 and Thomas Worsdell-designed GER Y14 0-6-0 No. 564 at Weybourne on the North Norfolk Railway in August 1989.

No. 69023 and Lambton colliery 0-6-2T No. 5 climb past Beckhole on the North Yorkshire Moors Railway on October 11, 1987

regular NYMR services but has seen frequent use on the line while also visiting a large number of heritage lines across the country.

Its livery in NELPG ownership has been the popular 'station pilot' livery used by BR for two members of the class which performed this duty at York and Newcastle, although this actually only lasted a year or so. Basically in NER green livery but with black wheels, No. 69023 carries its BR number plus the NER and BR emblems on the tank sides. It remains officially named *Joem* but the plate is carried inside the cab. It is now regarded as being based on the Wensleydale Railway. ∎

No. 69023 heads a coal train at Marley Hill on the Tanfield Railway on September 11, 2010.

No. 69023 passes the disused station of Wensley on the Wensleydale Railway on July 21, 2012. MAURICE BURNS

CHAPTER 7

Great Northern Railway

The contribution made to the history of steam preservation by the Great Northern Railway's four preserved steam locomotives cannot be overstated.

The Great Northern Railway was established by Act of Parliament in 1846. Its main line would eventually run from London King's Cross to Doncaster, becoming the southern part of the East Coast Main Line.

But the ECML did not initially run by the route we know today, the first section being built from Peterborough to Gainsborough via Boston. In fact the first part of the GNR, opened on March 1, 1848 was the Louth to Grimsby section of the East Lincolnshire Railway, which was leased to the GNR.

The GNR planned to run trains from London to Leeds and York but had to use running powers over the Lancashire & Yorkshire and Midland respectively to achieve this. It increased its involvement in West Yorkshire through running powers but without owning any lines beyond Askern Junction during the 1850s. Many of these small independent lines were eventually acquired by the GNR.

On August 7, 1850, the main line opened from a temporary station at Maiden Lane, London, to Peterborough, and the missing section of the ECML between Peterborough and Retford opened in 1852, as did the new London terminus at King's Cross. Doncaster locomotive works opened in 1853, replacing facilities at Boston.

A branch from Hitchin to Shepreth eventually got the GNR access to Cambridge, and access to Nottingham from Grantham over the Ambergate, Nottingham, Boston and Eastern Junction Railway and east from Grantham to Sleaford and Boston over the Boston, Sleaford and Midland Counties Railway expanded the GNR system, with further lines opening in due course.

GNR N2 0-6-2T No. 1744 and Large Atlantic No. 251 inside Barrow Hill Roundhouse.

GNR agreements with the Manchester Sheffield & Lincolnshire Railway also led to a GNR involvement in lines between Manchester and Liverpool, with the Midland Railway also having an interest, and from this an extensive joint line system grew later known as the Cheshire Lines Committee.

The main express trains on what became the ECML over the GNR, NER and NBR were the 10am departures from King's Cross and Edinburgh, which began running in June 1862, becoming known unofficially as the 'Flying Scotsman'.

The GNR's significance in terms of Britain's railway history cannot be overstated. It was to continue to dominate the development of the LNER particularly in motive power terms, and influence BR, in due course making a disproportionate contribution to the heritage railway industry. Yet few significant stretches of GNR trackage exists in preservation. Most of its closed routes are in rural Lincolnshire, where its system was destroyed in 1970. Today the Lincolnshire Wolds Railway has reinstated a short length of the GNR's East Lincolnshire line but little else exists in preservation.

The GNR's first locomotive superintendent, from 1850 to 1866, was Archibald Sturrock, born in Dundee in 1816. Although his father was an agent to the Bank of Scotland, the young Archibald took an apprenticeship at the Dundee Foundry at the age of 15. Here he was involved with the construction of a locomotive for the Dundee and Newtyle Railway and met Daniel Gooch, who would later become locomotive superintendent of the Great Western Railway.

Sturrock persuaded Gooch to offer him a post in the locomotive department of the GWR in 1840, and despite a difficult initial relationship with Brunel, Sturrock won his confidence and was appointed works manager at Swindon. It was a glowing reference from Brunel that helped secure Sturrock his job with the GNR.

On the GNR, Sturrock designed many classes of locomotives for passenger and the equally important goods traffic. He was involved right from the opening of the GN main line and established the GNR's reputation for reliable and comfortable passenger services.

After his retirement from the GNR, Sturrock had a long and active retirement in Doncaster, and died in London in 1909. Sturrock's engines were all built by outside contractors but he established workshops at Boston for heavy maintenance and repair. None of his designs survived into preservation.

Sturrock was succeeded as locomotive superintendent by Patrick Stirling, who had previously been locomotive superintendent of the Glasgow and South Western Railway. His brother, James Stirling, was also a locomotive engineer, while his son Matthew Stirling was chief mechanical engineer of the Hull and Barnsley Railway.

Stirling's most famous design was the 8ft Single, a 4-2-2 with 8ft diameter driving wheels, which set speed records during the Race to the North, with average train speeds between engine changes of more than 60mph even in 1895. Stirling's first Single No. 1 was set aside for preservation by the GNR on withdrawal in 1907 and has made a couple of notable appearances in steam in its long period of preservation.

Stirling's successor, Henry Alfred Ivatt became the GNR's chief mechanical engineer in 1896. He was born in Wentworth, Cambridgeshire, on September 16, 1851, and was educated at Liverpool College. Ivatt was apprenticed to John Ramsbottom at the LNWR's Crewe works at the age of 17 and progressed quickly through the ranks. He worked for the Great Southern and Western Railway at Inchicore in Ireland, being appointed locomotive engineer there in 1882.

Among Ivatt's notable achievements on the GNR was the introduction of the 4-4-2 (Atlantic) wheel arrangement to Britain, and he was also the first in the country to use Walschaerts valve

gear. Ivatt retired on December 2, 1911.

One of Ivatt's sons, George, also became a locomotive engineer and eventually chief mechanical engineer of the London Midland and Scottish Railway, and Henry's daughter Marjorie married Oliver Bulleid, assistant to Gresley at Doncaster and later chief mechanical engineer of the Southern Railway.

Two of Ivatt's celebrated Atlantics survived, both preserved by the LNER, the pioneer small Atlantic No. 990 *Henry Oakley*, and large Atlantic No. 251. One of Ivatt's more mundane tank engines; J13 (LNER J52) 0-6-0ST No. 1247 became Britain's first main line steam engine to be preserved by a private individual, back in 1959. It even saw main line action early in its preservation days.

Ivatt is also noted for several classes of 0-6-0 including the J6 which survived into the 1960s and the C12 4-4-2Ts, but none of these designs has been preserved.

Ivatt's successor was Herbert Nigel Gresley, destined to become one of Britain's most famous steam locomotive engineers. Gresley was born in Edinburgh but was raised in Netherseal, Derbyshire. After attending school in Sussex and at Marlborough College, like Ivatt before him, Gresley served his apprenticeship at Crewe works on the LNWR and continued to learn his trade under John Aspinall at Horwich on the L&YR, where he made rapid progress. He moved to the GNR, initially as carriage and wagon superintendent, but succeeded Ivatt as CME on October 1, 1911.

Although Gresley was known to admire Ivatt's Atlantics, his first designs were very different being powerful small-wheeled, big-boilered 2-6-0s. He is also noted for favouring three-cylinder designs, but differing from those on other railways by his preferred use of conjugated valve gear, where the three cylinders are driven by only two sets of Walschaerts valve gear. The Gresley conjugated valve gear was intended to produce smooth running and power with lower maintenance costs.

Sadly Gresley's pioneer locomotive designs, eventually becoming the LNER K2 and K3 2-6-0s did not survive into preservation. An example of his N2 0-6-2T still exists as does one of his first Pacifics, *Flying Scotsman*, ordered by the GNR but completed by the LNER after the 1923 Grouping.

GNR N2 0-6-2T No. 1744 departs from Keighley on the Worth Valley Railway on February 14, 2010, the first two vehicles in the train are ex-GNR ones.

GNR Stirling Single No. 1 on display at 'The Plant' at Doncaster.

4-2-2 No. 1

The Stirling Single was designed by Patrick Stirling for express passenger work on the GNR. With a single pair of 8ft diameter driving wheels, they were designed to haul up to 26 coaches at an average speed of 47mph. On his arrival at the GNR, Stirling set out to standardise the railway's rolling stock as there had been little standardisation under his predecessor, Sturrock.

Stirling established the locomotive works at Doncaster so that the GNR could start to build its own engines. He borrowed a single-wheeler from the Great Eastern Railway and, in 1868, designed two versions of 2-2-2 with 7ft 1in driving wheels. The GER designs were developed specifically for the GNR's high-speed expresses; Stirling using outside cylinders and a 4-2-2 wheel arrangement for extra stability at the front end at higher speeds.

Fifty-three Stirling 4-2-2s were built at Doncaster between 1870 and 1895. The GNR did not number its locomotives sequentially, instead using numbers freed up by withdrawn older locomotives.

As an indication of the capabilities of Stirling's express design, in the 1895 Race to the North, GNR Single No. 775 covered the 82 miles from Grantham to York in one hour 16 minutes, an average speed of 64.7mph.

With the arrival of the Ivatt Atlantics after 1898, the Singles began to be displaced from express services and withdrawals of the early engines began in 1899, but the last ones were used on secondary services until as late as 1916.

The first of the class, No. 1, was preserved by the GNR on withdrawal in 1907. Although normally stored at King's Cross shed or Doncaster works, it was put on show to the public occasionally and took part in the 1925 Stockton & Darlington centenary cavalcade in steam. This centenary led to the establishment of the York Railway Museum by the LNER and No. 1 was placed on permanent public exhibition.

It emerged from the museum in 1938 to take part in the LNER's publicity programme, hauling a GNR train on the GN main line, and also featuring in two public excursions, from King's Cross to Cambridge and Peterborough, becoming the first preserved British steam locomotive to haul a main line passenger train. It returned to the museum where it remained until closure in 1974, after which it moved to the new National Railway Museum.

A surprise was the decision to return it to steam in 1981-82, and it ran for just three weekends on the Great Central Railway. It also took part in a filming session on the North Yorkshire Moors Railway at Levisham and there was even talk of a main line run to Scarborough but this proved to be too ambitious.

No. 1 accelerates away from Loughborough on the Great Central Railway on May 8, 1982.

The Stirling Single on the turntable at the National Railway Museum at York.

C1 4-4-2 No. 990 *Henry Oakley*

The GNR small-boilered C1, designed by Henry Ivatt in 1897 was the first 4-4-2 to run in Great Britain. Twenty-two were built between 1898 and 1903 at Doncaster works and were commonly known as 'Klondykes' after the 1897 Klondike gold rush.

The 4-4-2 had first appeared in 1888 in the US, the natural development of the 4-4-0; the additional trailing truck not only supporting a larger firebox but improving the riding. The wheel arrangement became known as the Atlantic.

Ivatt's counterpart on the Lancashire & Yorkshire Railway, John Aspinall was also working on an Atlantic and construction of Ivatt's Atlantic was given a high priority by the GNR in order to beat the L&Y to it. Numbered 990 and named *Henry Oakley* after the general manager of the railway, it was outshopped from Doncaster in 1898, beating Aspinall's prototype by a few months. It was the only named engine on the GNR until Gresley's first Pacific emerged in 1922.

The first production Atlantics entered service in 1900 and proved fast runners, sometimes having to be held back on less well-maintained sections of track. Ivatt set the boiler design as a priority but the enginemen felt that the cylinders were no match for the boiler. These first Atlantics had to be driven harder than was desirable to produce satisfactory performances.

After the Grouping this class became LNER C2, whereas the later large-boilered engines were class C1. In 1937, No. 990 was withdrawn and in view of its importance in the development of ECML locomotive design, was restored to original condition by the LNER and put on show in the railway museum at York.

It was taken out of the museum in 1953 along with its larger cousin No. 251 to work 'The Plant Centenarian' railtour from King's Cross to Doncaster in September, organised by a Retford businessman by the name of Alan Pegler.

It returned to the museum where it stayed until its closure but when moved to the new National Railway Museum in York, it was not put on display. Instead it was prepared for an appearance in steam at the 1975 Stockton & Darlington cavalcade at Shildon. It even travelled from York to Shildon along the ECML under its own steam, hauling Stirling Single No. 1.

A working visit to the Keighley & Worth Valley Railway in 1977-78 was unfortunately cut short by boiler problems just before No. 990 was due to travel to Doncaster works. It was duly hauled there by No. 4472 *Flying Scotsman,* after which it went on show at the NRM. It was relocated to Bressingham in Norfolk in 1997 but has never been returned to steam since.

During its all-too-brief second period of active preservation, No. 990 *Henry Oakley* departs from Oakworth on the Keighley & Worth Valley Railway in 1978. DAVE RODGERS

No. 990 *Henry Oakley* at the Boston 150 celebrations on September 12, 1998.

Henry Oakley in the Rail 150 cavalcade at Shildon on August 31, 1975.

GNR Atlantic No. 990 *Henry Oakley* is towed past Goosehill Junction, Normanton by LNER A3 Pacific No. 4472 *Flying Scotsman* en route from Keighley to Doncaster on June 16, 1978.

GNR Large Atlantic No. 251 at Barrow Hill Roundhouse.

C1 4-4-2 No. 251

Following on from the success of his first Atlantics, Ivatt built the large-boilered version for the GNR. In December 1902, No. 251 appeared from Doncaster, the design being a natural development of the 'Klondyke' with a much larger boiler. The GNR classified both as C1, but the LNER classified the large-boilered version as C1 and the small-boilered one C2.

The large boiler and firebox was a result of Ivatt's belief that the ability to boil water was the main criterion of an engine's performance, but he still did not fit correspondingly larger cylinders, and although 20 more C1s were built in 1904, they were still not right. The wide firebox left no space for the normal screw reversing gear, so a lever was used, which was hard to operate, especially at speed.

Ivatt experimented with several variations to the design even including four-cylinder compounds with a mixture of Walschaerts and Stephenson valve gear. Between 1905 and 1908, 60 C1s were built with simple expansion, but with the lever reversing gear replaced by a screw reverser accommodated by redesigning the firebox, which was deepened at the front, making firing easier. Alteration of earlier engines started in 1925 and was completed by 1933.

Ivatt's last development was the fitting of piston valves and Schmidt superheaters to the last 10 C1s built in 1910, with an increase in cylinder diameter from 18.75in to 20in. With superheating, the boiler pressure was decreased from 175psi to 150psi. This finally produced a successful engine but still with room for improvement.

No further Atlantics were built after Gresley succeeded Ivatt as the GNR's chief mechanical engineer in 1911, but Gresley continued to make improvements to the C1s, which then sufficed for GNR express services until Gresley introduced his A1 Pacifics in 1922.

It was under Gresley that Robinson superheaters were gradually fitted to all the Atlantics by 1927, the 24-row type replaced by 32-row by 1934, after which they performed their best work, being capable of feats such as taking a train of 17 coaches over 60 miles at an average speed of 64mph.

During the war, the C1s were seen more often north of York and even Newcastle, but their condition deteriorated quickly and withdrawal started in 1943, accelerated by the introduction of Thompson's new B1 4-6-0s. Just 17 C1s survived into BR days, the last one, No. 62822 being withdrawn in November 1950.

The first C1, No. 251, was preserved by the LNER just before Nationalisation and put on display in York museum. It partnered No. 990 on the 'Plant Centenarian' from King's Cross to Doncaster in September 1953 and hauled two further railtours in September 1954, both in tandem with GCR Director 4-4-0 No. 62663 *Prince Albert*, one from Retford to Liverpool and the second from Leeds to Basingstoke for the Farnborough air show. It returned to the museum but has not been steamed since and is currently on display at Barrow Hill Roundhouse.

J13 0-6-0ST No. 1247

The GNR J14 was Stirling's last saddletank design and appeared in 1892, designed mainly for shunting the larger yards on the GN system. The J14 had a domeless boiler five inches longer than that of his earlier saddletank. Fifty-two were built up to 1897, by Neilson & Co, or at Doncaster.

Seventeen were built with condensing gear for operating over the Metropolitan Widened Lines and 10 more had the gear retrofitted in 1900, though some had it removed when they moved to Leeds and Doncaster.

In 1897, Ivatt introduced a version with a domed larger-diameter boiler, and this became GNR J13. Eighty-five were built up to 1899 and were to become LNER class J52. They were to be found right across the system. The GNR rebuilt three J14s as J13s and the LNER rebuilt the rest by 1932.

Withdrawals of the J52s took place over a long period from 1936 to 1961, halted during the war but accelerated once diesel shunters arrived in quantity.

One class member, No. 68846, was painted in lined mixed-traffic black livery for an exhibition at Hatfield in 1957, along with recently withdrawn C12 4-4-2T No. 67357 and, after the exhibition, the J52 was adopted as King's Cross shed pilot, for which it retained its lined-out livery and immaculate condition. No. 68846 became the first main line locomotive to be privately

GNR J13 0-6-0ST No. 1247 heads the 'Blue Belle' railtour from London Bridge to the Bluebell Railway at Horsted Keynes on April 1, 1962. COLOUR-RAIL.COM 102395

No. 1247 climbs past Beckhole on the North Yorkshire Moors Railway on April 22, 1978.

No. 1247 works a goods train under the motorway bridge on the Middleton Railway in Leeds on June 23, 1990.

preserved when it was purchased from BR by Captain Bill Smith RN in 1959. On withdrawal and purchase, it hauled a two-coach train including the GNR engineer's saloon from King's Cross to Marshmoor on May 7, 1959, where it was based in a private siding and restoration to GNR livery as No. 1247 commenced.

After a light engine run to Peterborough on June 1, 1959, No. 1247 became the first privately preserved steam engine to haul a main line railtour, an SLS members-only brakevan special on the freight-only line from Hatfield to St Albans Abbey on June 17, 1961. More ambitious outings followed culminating in the engine heading 'The Blue Belle' from London Bridge to the Bluebell Railway on April 1, 1962.

On March 4-6, 1965 it moved under its own steam to the Keighley & Worth Valley Railway where it saw occasional use before reopening in 1968. Before the railway reopened it joined the growing collection of steam locomotives at the Standard Gauge Steam Trust's centre at Tyseley in Birmingham, where it also saw little use until moved to the North Yorkshire Moors Railway in November 1974. It was returned to steam in March 1975, and although rather small, it saw regular passenger service on the line for a while.

In 1980 it was donated by Captain Smith to the National Railway Museum, arriving for display in January 1981. Still in good condition, it was transferred to Hull on September 25, 1985, where it was returned to steam once more in 1990 by the Humberside Locomotive Preservation Group under the leadership of Tom Tighe.

No. 1247 departs from Sheringham during the first North Norfolk Railway steam gala on September 19, 1993, passing LMS 3F 'Jinty' 0-6-0T No. 47383.

GNR J52 0-6-0ST No. 68846 running as unlined black No. 68867 heads a goods train at Cranmore on the East Somerset Railway on November 18, 1995.

No. 1247 stands on the turntable at the Sacramento Railway Museum, incongruously alongside Amtrak Superliner stock on May 12, 1991.

Returning to the NRM in June 1990, it was steamed at York and occasionally loaned to other railways, but it made its longest journey ever in 1991, appearing in steam at a prestigious event at the Sacramento Railway Museum in California.

A new deal saw it move to the East Somerset Railway on September 1, 1995, where a repaint to its BR King's Cross shed pilot black livery as No. 68846 took place and it continued to appear at other railway events, even being reunited with the GNR engineer's saloon that had had an expensive refurbishment on the Bluebell Railway.

Yet another overhaul followed, this time by Bill Parker at the Flour Mill workshop in the Forest of Dean where it arrived on September 15, 1998. Now under Bill's control on behalf of the NRM, it started its next round of travels at the Great Central Railway (Nottingham) at Ruddington in July 1999.

Since its retirement from these duties after 45 years of preservation mostly spent as a working locomotive, it has spent its longest period yet as a static exhibit, mostly at the Locomotion museum at Shildon, where it has regained its familiar GNR livery and identity.

In King's Cross shed pilot livery, No. 68846 approaches Horsted Keynes on the Bluebell Railway with the GNR engineers' saloon on June 21, 1997.

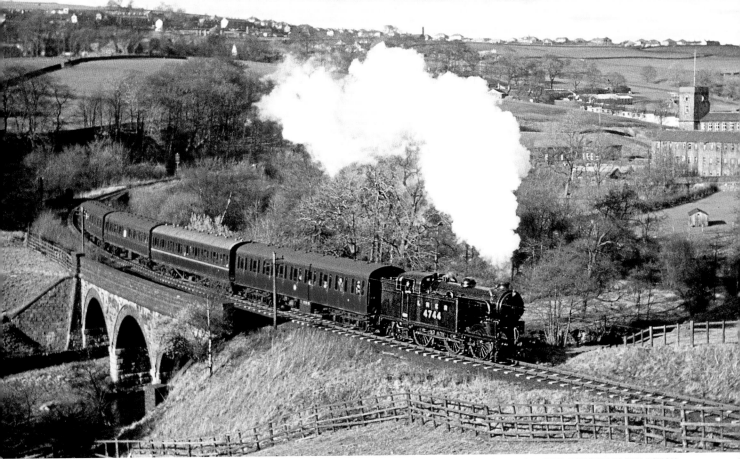

GNR N2 0-6-2T No. 4744 crosses Mytholmes viaduct on the Keighley & Worth Valley Railway in its early days of operation. PAUL CHANCELLOR COLLECTION

N2 0-6-2T No. 1744

With the completion of the final batch of Ivatt's N1 0-6-2Ts, the GNR did not require any further suburban tank locomotives until after the First World War. Gresley considered a 2-6-2T, and a 2-6-4T, but an improved 0-6-2T was accepted for development, and the GNR N2 0-6-2T was introduced in 1920. Interestingly Gresley much later designed a 2-6-2T and his successor, Thompson, designed a 2-6-4T for heavier suburban work.

Designed mainly for working suburban trains, the N2's main duties were from King's Cross and Moorgate, often hauling one or two Quad-Art sets of articulated suburban coaches, but they also hauled some empty stock trains from King's Cross. Some were fitted with condensing apparatus for working on the Metropolitan Railway Widened Lines between King's Cross and Moorgate.

The N2s were an immediate success and there were to be four main variants, although the sub-classifications were not used until about 1928. The N2/2 batch was built in 1925 by Beyer, Peacock & Co, and were the first LNER Group Standard N2s, with left-hand drive and a tall chimney, but no condensers.

After trials in 1924 in the Glasgow area, 12 new N2s were ordered for Scotland mainly for suburban services and in 1927 many King's Cross N2s joined them in Scotland and Dunfermline, Haymarket, and North Berwick all acquired the class for the first time.

The N2s were never very popular in Scotland and as the V1 2-6-2Ts became available, 28 N2s were permanently moved back to London and the remaining Scottish N2s did very little for the rest of their lives.

Two N2s were tried in the West Riding in 1926, followed by a permanent allocation to Bradford and Ardsley in 1931. The West Riding N2s were found to have much quicker acceleration than the N1s, but they were less suited to the sharp curves in the area. From September 1937 to August 1939, the high-speed streamlined 'West Riding Limited' was hauled between Bradford Exchange and Leeds Central stations by a pair of N2s. By 1945 though, all of the West Riding N2s had returned to London or moved to Nottingham.

All 107 of the class survived into British Railways

In LNER black livery, No. 4744 and B1 4-6-0 No. 1306 *Mayflower* depart from Rothley on the Great Central Railway on May 27, 1979.

GNR N2 0-6-2T No. 69523 in BR black livery with a train of LNER teak TPO coaches at Loughborough Central on the Great Central Railway.

ownership and in 1948, most were in the King's Cross area, although Colwick had five, Neasden three, and 16 remained in Scotland.

When diesels arrived at King's Cross in the 1950s, the N2s were gradually withdrawn, some acting as station pilots, and some moving briefly to New England. The last 13 of the class were withdrawn in 1962, and one of these, No. 69523 was purchased by the Gresley Society and initially kept at the NCB locomotive shed at Harworth Colliery in South Yorkshire. A move via Walton Colliery to the Keighley & Worth Valley Railway was completed in January 1965 and the engine worked regularly on the line at early open days in LNER livery as No. 4744, plus making an appearance in the filming of The Railway Children in 1970 hauling the 'Scotch Express'.

It moved to the Great Central Railway on November 2, 1975, and returned to steam in 1978. It has remained based at Loughborough but has worked sometimes for long periods elsewhere, including an appearance in the 'Steam on the Met' event in 1994.

It was turned out in GNR apple green livery in 2009 as No. 1744 and has been appropriately matched with the Midland & Great Northern Railway's restored set of Gresley Quad-Art coaches on the North Norfolk Railway. ∎

In GNR livery, N2 0-6-2T No. 1744 approaches Weybourne on the North Norfolk Railway with the restored set of Gresley quad-art coaches.

Midland & Great Northern Joint Railway

Affectionately known as the 'Muddle and Get Nowhere' to generations of passengers and enthusiasts, the M&GN was owned jointly by the Midland Railway, and the Great Northern Railway.

Running from an end-on junction with the MR branch from Saxby Junction on the Nottingham main line to Great Yarmouth via South Lynn and Melton Constable, the M&GN's main line had branches running from Sutton Bridge to Peterborough; and from Melton Constable to Cromer and to Norwich.

It was formed in 1893 by the amalgamation of many smaller local lines, and gave its joint owners access to the ports of East Anglia, while enabling them to develop what was to become a lucrative source of revenue from holiday-makers coming from London and the industrial Midlands to the east coast resorts.

Its opening ended the GER's monopoly of East

Anglian railways. Much of the route was single-track, with surprisingly steep gradients, but goods traffic was heavy, and on the busiest days in the holiday season the line could see up to 100 trains a day with resultant operating problems.

The heart of the system was Melton Constable with the M&GN's engineering centre meaning the village earned the nickname 'the Crewe of North Norfolk'.

For more than 40 years William Marriott served the M&GN and its predecessors, joining the staff of the original contractors in 1881, and finally becoming traffic manager as well as locomotive superintendent in 1919, before retiring in 1924. He is commemorated in the name of the Marriott's Way footpath, much of which follows the trackbed of the M&GN Norwich line.

The M&GN mainly used MR or GNR locomotive designs but once part of the LNER, the M&GN engines

were all quickly scrapped; a sole survivor being a boiler from a Hudswell Clarke 4-4-0T. Although there have been plans for this to form the basis of a new-build project, it seems more likely that it could be used on a new GCR engine with a similar type of boiler.

For much of the company's existence, its locomotives were painted light golden brown, but from 1922 the goods engines were painted dark brown, followed by the rest of the locomotives in 1929.

The M&GN was one of the first major railway closures with virtually the entire system being abandoned in February 1959. There is as much of the M&GN now preserved as there is in Network Rail use. Cromer to Sheringham is part of the national network while Sheringham to Holt is now part of the North Norfolk Railway, the two five-mile long surviving sections having been reconnected in 2010 for the first time in 40 years. In 2009 on the 50th anniversary of its closure to passengers the station at Whitwell & Reepham on the Norwich branch was reopened.

A surprising number of other M&GN stations and signalboxes survive, often in remote locations but little rolling stock can now be seen.

A Beyer Peacock 4-4-2T in M&GN ochre livery is featured on a bus stop at Melton Constable which also incorporates two spandrels from the station roof.

LEFT: The Midland & Great Northern Joint Railway Society's GER J15 0-6-0 No. 65462 leaves Sheringham on the North Norfolk Railway on the preserved part of the M&GN.

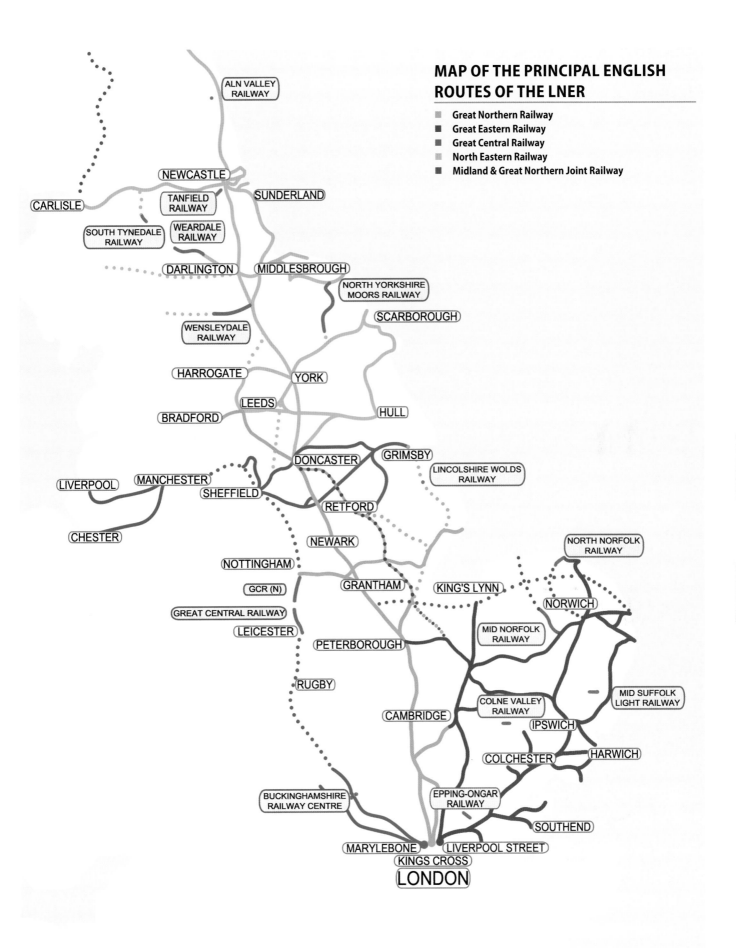

MAP OF THE PRINCIPAL ENGLISH ROUTES OF THE LNER

- Great Northern Railway
- Great Eastern Railway
- Great Central Railway
- North Eastern Railway
- Midland & Great Northern Joint Railway

ALN VALLEY RAILWAY

CARLISLE

NEWCASTLE

SUNDERLAND

TANFIELD RAILWAY

SOUTH TYNEDALE RAILWAY

WEARDALE RAILWAY

DARLINGTON

MIDDLESBROUGH

NORTH YORKSHIRE MOORS RAILWAY

SCARBOROUGH

WENSLEYDALE RAILWAY

HARROGATE

YORK

LEEDS

BRADFORD

HULL

GRIMSBY

DONCASTER

LINCOLNSHIRE WOLDS RAILWAY

LIVERPOOL

MANCHESTER

SHEFFIELD

RETFORD

CHESTER

NEWARK

NOTTINGHAM

NORTH NORFOLK RAILWAY

GCR (N)

GRANTHAM

KING'S LYNN

NORWICH

GREAT CENTRAL RAILWAY

MID NORFOLK RAILWAY

LEICESTER

PETERBOROUGH

MID SUFFOLK LIGHT RAILWAY

RUGBY

COLNE VALLEY RAILWAY

CAMBRIDGE

IPSWICH

COLCHESTER

HARWICH

BUCKINGHAMSHIRE RAILWAY CENTRE

EPPING-ONGAR RAILWAY

SOUTHEND

MARYLEBONE

LIVERPOOL STREET

KINGS CROSS

LONDON

CHAPTER 8

Great Eastern Railway

The GER is well represented in preservation by several heritage lines and a representative selection of steam power.

The GER was formed in 1862 by the amalgamation of the Eastern Counties Railway with a number of smaller railways. Its 1200 route miles served virtually the whole of East Anglia, much of it was extremely rural but it also served the East London suburban area, and it was this network that was the most heavily used steam-hauled commuter system in the world in the early years of the 20th century.

The ECR's original London terminus was opened at Shoreditch in East London on July 1, 1840 and renamed Bishopsgate on July 27, 1847, but when Bishopsgate closed to passengers a new London terminus at Liverpool Street was opened by the GER on February 2, 1874.

Today the preserved parts of the GER are the Mid-Norfolk, Epping-Ongar and Colne Valley railways. There is also the East Anglian Railway Museum at Chappell & Wakes Colne, while miniature lines also run on GER trackbeds including the Wells & Walsingham and Bure Valley railways.

The majority of the GER's locomotives were built at Stratford works, a vast complex that included the running sheds and part of which is now buried under today's Stratford International station. The GER's early locomotive superintendents were Sinclair from 1862, Johnson from 1866, Adams from 1873 and Bromley from 1878. In 1881, Bromley was succeeded by T W Worsdell. He was born in Liverpool in 1838, the eldest son of Nathaniel Worsdell, who constructed the Liverpool & Manchester Railway's first carriages. On T W's return from the US in 1871, he became the works manager at Crewe on the LNWR under F W Webb. His stay with the GER was though, and he moved on to become locomotive superintendent of the NER in 1885.

Worsdell's early two-cylinder compounds for the GER were not particularly successful but his 0-6-0s and 2-4-2Ts became classic GER and NER designs for the next 20 years, with T W Worsdell being particularly remembered for the Y14 (LNER J15) 0-6-0s on the GER and the C class (J21) 0-6-0s on the NER.

Worsdell's successor on the GER, James Holden, was more successful. He was born in Whitstable, Kent on July 26, 1837, and was apprenticed to his uncle, Edward Fletcher and in 1865, joined the GWR, where he eventually became chief assistant to William Dean. He was appointed locomotive superintendent of the GER in 1885, and held the post until 1907. He was a Quaker who also disapproved of trade unionism.

Holden reorganised Stratford works, and by introducing a degree of standardisation, took Stratford to an exceptionally high position among British locomotive works in the speed and efficiency of its locomotive production. He was particularly noted for once erecting a Y14 0-6-0 in just nine hours 47 minutes and pioneered the use of oil firing for steam locomotives.

Although he improved existing designs, in his first year at Stratford, four designs were introduced; a 2-4-2T, an 0-6-0T, an 0-6-0 goods and the T19 2-4-0 express passenger class, which was to prove the mainstay of GER main line passenger services for many years. Although initially against the use of front bogies, Holden was responsible for the Claud Hamilton 4-4-0, and also designed the unique but shortlived 'Decapod' 0-10-0T for suburban services.

Holden was succeeded by his son, Stephen, in 1908. He was born at Saltney, Cheshire in 1870 and joined the GER at Stratford at the age of 16 and studied under his father for four years.

Stephen's designs tended to be a continuation of his father's products, partly as Stratford kept the same chief draughtsman, E S Tiddeman, and some even perpetuated T W Worsdell's products. The most notable new design was the enlargement of the Claud Hamilton 4-4-0 into the S69 4-6-0 in 1911, the first six-coupled express locomotive to run on the GER.

Stephen Holden resigned from the GER in October 1912 and died at Rochester in 1918, seven years before his father.

Several of James Holden's designs have survived but not the Claud Hamilton 4-4-0, which had all been rebuilt by the 1950s and were not therefore considered suitable for the National Collection. Similarly, Stephen Holden's 4-6-0 design was rebuilt by Gresley into the LNER B12 and none survive in original form.

In 1912, Alfred John Hill took over to become the GER's last chief mechanical engineer. His best-known design is the L77 0-6-2T for the Liverpool Street suburban services, which as LNER class N7, was perpetuated by Gresley after the Grouping.

GER N7 0-6-2T No. 69621 crosses Chappell & Wakes Colne viaduct on the Stour Valley branch with a test train in December 1992.
GEOFF SILCOCK

No. 229 at North Woolwich. MALCOLM BATTEN

209 class 0-4-0ST No. 229

Only eight GER 209 class 0-4-0STs were built, and had flat-topped, instead of round-topped, tanks, being referred to as 'Ogee'. Originally, two were purchased from Neilsons in 1874 to one of its standard designs, to shunt in the goods yard at Devonshire Street and at Canning Town, with its tight curves and weight restrictions, and two more followed in 1876. In 1894-1895 these four locomotives were rebuilt by Holden with new boilers, steam brakes, and covered cabs.

In 1897 two new locomotives were built at Stratford, almost identical to the rebuilt ones, and two more were built, also at Stratford, six years later. These were used at Colchester, Lowestoft Harbour and Stratford carriage works.

However, four of them were withdrawn or sold by the GER, the remaining four becoming LNER class Y5. The last one, No. 7230, the Stratford carriage works shunter, was renumbered 8081 in 1944; and just survived into BR ownership in 1948 but was scrapped early that year before it could receive its BR number. During the 1930s it carried lined black livery, and attended many railway exhibitions in former GER territory.

The GER only ever sold one locomotive out of service, and that was 209 class No. 229 in 1917. As part of the First World War effort, No. 229 moved in 1917 to the Admiralty's National Shipyard No. 1 at Chepstow. After the cessation of hostilities, a

private company was formed to buy and run the yard retaining all fixtures and fittings, all passing to Glasgow-based Fairfield Shipbuilding & Engineering Co a few years later. Finally retired in the 1960s, the locomotive was bought by Bill Parker and moved to the Dean Forest Railway in 1982. It spent a period on display at the North Woolwich Railway Museum from 1984 until closure of the museum, and is now under overhaul to working order at Bill Parker's Flour Mill workshop in the Forest of Dean.

No. 229 is lifted out of the museum at North Woolwich on June 5, 2008 for the journey to the Forest of Dean. GEOFF SILCOCK

T26 2-4-0 No. 490

James Holden's T26 2-4-0 was a development of his earlier T19 express engine but with much smaller 5ft 8in driving wheels and intended for mixed-traffic work. The LNER classified them E4.

Between 1891 and 1896, 90 were built with 140psi pressure boilers. From 1898 some were rebuilt with new 160psi pressure boilers and when an additional 10 were built in 1902 these were fitted with the new boilers as standard.

The GER used air brakes but, when introduced, more than half the T26s were additionally fitted with vacuum brake ejectors for operating over the lines of other railway companies. T26s were often used on passenger trains to the Norfolk coast, particularly Wells and Cromer, before the Claud Hamilton 4-4-0s took over.

On introduction, the T26s were painted in the standard GER livery of ultramarine blue with vermilion lining. From 1915 they were not given a top coat and ran in French grey undercoat with some black lining.

Eighteen survived into BR ownership in 1948, the last being withdrawn in 1959, making them the last 2-4-0s to work in Britain. The last survivor, BR No. 62785 was associated with the Mildenhall branch and when withdrawn on December 5, 1959 was selected for official preservation and restored to original condition and livery as No. 490 at Stratford works.

It was put on display in Clapham museum on December 11, 1960 and moved by rail to the new NRM in 1974 but in July 1985 was sent on loan to the Bressingham steam museum in Norfolk. It has never been steamed in preservation.

GER T26 2-4-0 No. 490 at the Bressingham steam museum.

GER S56 0-6-0T No. 87 on display at the National Railway Museum at York.

S56 0-6-0T No. 87

James Holden designed the T18, which was the first successful GER 0-6-0T and used for shunting. These were followed by the larger R24s of which 140 were built, 100 being intended for passenger duties, fitted with screw reversers, Westinghouse brakes and, in many cases, condensing gear.

The Holden S56 0-6-0T was a development of the R24, being almost identical, but with higher boiler pressure and larger water tanks. Twenty were built at Stratford in 1904 and passed to the

LNER in 1923. Along with some rebuilt R24s, they received the LNER classification J69, while the original R24s became J67.

Most of the J69s and J67s were allocated to Stratford, with 121 being there at the Grouping, but both passenger and shunting locomotives could also be found at Colchester, Ipswich, Cambridge, King's Lynn, and Peterborough East, with the passenger versions also at Norwich, Yarmouth, and Lowestoft. The Stratford passenger locomotives were mainly used on the 'Jazz' suburban services to Enfield Town and Chingfield, which were heavy and very intensive services.

However in 1925, the new N7 0-6-2Ts displaced many of the passenger 0-6-0Ts from the heavier duties and 59 of the J69s were converted to shunting locomotives by fitting lever reverse gear and removing any condensing gear, and they found themselves shunting in all parts of the LNER system, even in Scotland. Some stayed on the GE and continued to operate as passenger pilots, and hauling occasional passenger services.

Before the Second World War, 12 J69s were withdrawn and 13 were sold to the WD in October 1940, and used on the Melbourne and Longmoor military railways. In BR days, No. 68619 was painted in GER blue livery and used as Liverpool Street station pilot for a while. Postwar withdrawals started in 1953; the last J67 was withdrawn in 1958, and the last J69 in 1962.

J69 No. 68633 was selected for preservation in the National Collection and on withdrawal was restored at Stratford as S56 No. 87 in GER blue livery and put on display in the Museum of British Transport at Clapham. It was moved in 1974 to the National Railway Museum at York but has never steamed in preservation. Despite rumours of it being put on display in the concourse at Liverpool Street, this has not happened and the engine is on loan to the Bressingham Steam Museum in Norfolk.

GER J17 0-6-0 No. 8217 in LNER livery at Barrow Hill Roundhouse.

G58 0-6-0 No. 1217

The G58 0-6-0 was designed by James Holden for freight traffic. The class consisted partly of new locomotives built in 1905-1911 and partly of rebuilds of some of the 60 earlier F48s, originally built in 1900-1903, then the largest 0-6-0s in Britain and a freight version of the Claud Hamilton 4-4-0.

The rebuilding was continued by the LNER; those retaining round-top fireboxes were classified J16, and those built or rebuilt, with Belpaire fireboxes were classified J17, but as rebuilding continued, the J16s were extinct by 1932.

The original standard GE low roof cabs were replaced by 7in wider cabs with higher roofs but they remained wooden and only five J17s finally received steel roofs in the 1950s.

All 90 locomotives were initially allocated to March and Peterborough for use on coal and heavy goods trains and continued to be concentrated at these sheds until around 1931, when they started to be displaced by larger engines and found themselves working from other sheds on different duties.

In 1942, many J17s were moved to the former M&GN line to replace withdrawn M&GN locomotives and 17 were fitted for

hauling passenger services. For goods engines, the J17s performed reasonably well but after Nationalisation, they were displaced by new LMS Ivatt 4MT 2-6-0s.

In 1948, 89 J17s passed to BR and were given the numbers 65500-65589. No. 8200 had been destroyed in a German V2 rocket explosion at Stratford in November 1944; a second was withdrawn in 1953, and the last in 1962.

One of the last J17s to be withdrawn was No. 65567 which had been selected for preservation in the National Collection, representing an original Holden design, the Claud Hamilton not qualifying because all had been extensively rebuilt. It was one of the lucky engines to receive external restoration at Doncaster works to original livery as GER No. 1217 but there was nowhere to exhibit it and it went into store at Hellifield. It set off from there on January 19, 1968 to move to Preston Park where it arrived on March 17, after a troublesome journey with overheating bearings.

It finally went on public display in East Anglia at Bressingham in 1972 but moved to the National Railway Museum at York in 1985. It has never been steamed in preservation and is currently on loan to the Barrow Hill Roundhouse at Staveley, carrying LNER livery as No. 8217.

J15 0-6-0 No. 65462

The Y14 was designed by T W Worsdell for freight and passenger duties and proved very successful at both, being light enough to work over virtually all routes on the GER system. They were introduced in July 1883, largely in response to the need for additional motive power for the increase in coal traffic after the opening of the Great Eastern's joint line with the Great Northern from Doncaster. The GER continued to build them right up to 1913 with little design change, the class eventually totalling 289. Holden had tried to improve on the design at one stage without success.

On December 10-11, 1891, Stratford works built Y14 No. 930 and had it in steam with a coat of grey primer in nine hours 47 minutes, halving the previous record set at Crewe and it remains a world record. The locomotive ran 5000 miles on Peterborough to London coal trains before coming back to the works for the final coat of paint. It lasted 40 years and ran a total of 1,127,750 miles.

During the First World War, 43 of the 0-6-0s served in France and Belgium, one of which was withdrawn on its return as being beyond repair. There were further withdrawals before the Grouping and the LNER inherited 272 Y14s, spread right across the GE lines.

All the Y14s were built with a stovepipe chimney but this was replaced in LNER days by a cast chimney with a small lip. As with all GER classes, the Y14 had cabs with low wooden roofs covered with canvas but these were replaced in LNER days by higher arched sheet metal roofs. The last of the original batch of J15s, No. 7690 was sold in 1938 to Bairds and Scottish Steel Company in Lanarkshire and was not broken up until around 1960.

The J15s continued to be withdrawn by the LNER and were increasingly confined to branch line services but it was not until the introduction of Gresley's much larger J39 0-6-0 that the J15s were displaced from their main line duties, and 127 survived to enter BR service. The last four were withdrawn on September 16, 1962, right at the end of steam on the Great Eastern section.

One of the last ones in service, No. 65462 was purchased by the Midland & Great Northern Joint Railway Society, which had been formed to save a section of the M&GN which had been closed almost

After overhaul at Weybourne, the J15 appeared in GER grey livery as Y14 No. 564 in 1978.

GER J15 0-6-0 No. 65462 departs from Weybourne on the North Norfolk Railway as N7 0-6-2T No. 69621 climbs towards Kelling Heath.

Back in very familiar territory though much changed, No. 65462 visited the reinstated Whitemoor yard at March on May 23, 2004, carrying the identity of March-based No. 65420. PAUL BASON

In LNER livery, J15 No. 7564 departs from Sheringham on the North Norfolk Railway with Quad-Art stock, passing LMS 'Black Five' 4-6-0 No. 45337.

GER N7 0-6-2T No. 69621 at the East Anglian Railway Museum at Chappell & Wakes Colne. GEOFF SILCOCK

in its entirety in 1959; the country's biggest railway closure to date. The society was able to purchase the J15 along with B12 4-6-0 No. 61572, which were moved from Stratford and stored at the LMR's Devons Road diesel depot in East London.

In 1964, the Sheringham to Melton Constable section of the M&GN was closed by BR, and the M&GN Society set its sights on preserving the line running west from Sheringham. After a period in store at March, its two locomotives arrived at Sheringham on June 6, 1967. The J15 returned to steam briefly in 1969 in GER blue livery and worked occasional members' trains. A more thorough overhaul saw it enter regular passenger service in GER grey livery in 1978.

In 2002 it emerged from another overhaul at Weybourne, now in BR livery, but at the end of its boiler certificate in 2012, as LNER No. 7564, it was withdrawn for its third major refurbishment in preservation, which will see it return to original GER condition as a Y14.

N7 0-6-2T No. 69621

By 1914 the GER had introduced some modern ideas such as Belpaire boilers, superheating and piston valves for express and goods engines and A J Hill turned his attention to doing likewise for the suburban tank engines. Unusually for an inside-cylinder engine, his L77 0-6-2T had piston valves and Walschaerts valve gear. Of the first two engines, No. 1000 had a Robinson superheater, but No. 1001 was unsuperheated for comparison. No. 1000 was painted 'photographic grey' for official portraits, while No. 1001 was destined to be the only one of the class to carry GER blue livery, as the plain wartime grey livery was introduced shortly afterwards, and lasted until well after the Grouping.

The engines proved to be a success, but the intervention of the First World War meant that further engines could not be built until 1920. A final 10 were ordered at the very end of the GER's independent existence, and these were delivered as LNER Nos. 990E-999E in 1923-24, No. 999E proving to be the last locomotive to be constructed at Stratford works.

The LNER designated them N7, and Gresley adopted the class as a standard design, along with his own N2 0-6-2T designed for the GNR suburban lines. Although very similar designs, the larger driving wheels of the N2s were better suited to the GN line, which had more widely spaced stations, giving the opportunity for fast running, while

No. 69621 departs from Harrow-on-the-Hill for Amersham on May 17, 1992 during London Transport's Steam on the Met event.

No. 69621 is on main line duties working shuttles at an open day at Colchester on August 26, 1991.

on the GE system, the closer spacing of the stations meant that rapid acceleration was of greater importance. The N7s continued to be built in several batches by different builders with various design differences.

Initially, the LNER-built N7s were used in various areas, but by the 1930s all were in London; the Westinghouse air-braked engines on the GE section and 20 vacuum-braked engines on the GN.

The majority of the GE engines remained on the suburban services until electrified in 1960, after which a few were retained at Stratford for the North Woolwich line.

In September 1962, No. 69621, originally No. 999E, the last engine to be built at Stratford, was purchased for preservation by R F Youell, the intention being that it would be used on commercial coal traffic on the Middleton Railway in Leeds. However, it remained in store at Neville Hill shed until it was towed to the Stour Valley Railway at Chappell & Wakes Colne on September 2, 1973 for restoration to working order. It was returned to steam at what had become the East Anglian Railway Museum in August 1989. Main line certified it worked some shuttles at places such as Southend and Colchester and even ventured on to the Stour Valley branch on two weekends in 1992.

June 2000 saw the engine move to the North Norfolk Railway where it was a regular performer for several years but it has also seen service on many other heritage lines, latterly the Churnet Valley Railway. Its boiler certificate expired in 2014. ∎

GER N7 0-6-2T No. 69621 heads a train of box vans through Wansford on the Nene Valley Railway on April 30, 1993.

No. 69621 arrives at Holt on the North Norfolk Railway.

No. 69621 at Sheringham with newly-restored Gresley Quad-Art coaches on the North Norfolk Railway.

No. 69621 is a long way from home at Garthydwr on the Llangollen Railway on October 12, 2008.

No. 69621 under repair at Weybourne shed on the North Norfolk Railway.

No. 69621 departs from Consall on the Churnet Valley Railway in 2013. DICK MANTON

CHAPTER 9

Great Central Railway

A small part of the last main line built in Britain has now become the only double track heritage line.

RIGHT: GCR 11F 4-4-0 No. 506 *Butler-Henderson* at Loughborough on the Great Central Railway on May 8, 1982.

BELOW: GCR O4 2-8-0 No. 63601 departs from Loughborough Central on the double track Great Central Railway.

The Manchester, Sheffield and Lincolnshire Railway was formed in 1847 by amalgamation of the Sheffield, Ashton-under-Lyne and Manchester Railway, which had opened between Manchester and Sheffield via Woodhead in 1845, and two proposed lines in Lincolnshire.

One of the Lincolnshire lines was completed from Grimsby and New Holland to Sheffield via Lincoln and Gainsborough in 1849. The first section of this line, from Grimsby to New Holland, had opened the same day as the GNR's first line, from Grimsby to Louth. The MSLR and GNR also crossed near Retford, with a shared station, and the GNR had running powers on MSLR tracks into Sheffield, giving it access to Manchester and Liverpool, while also giving the MS&LR access to London.

The early history of the MSLR was complicated and acrimonious as the railway crossed the territories of many competing companies, and any attempt to cooperate with one company tended to alienate two or three others. By working with the LNWR, LYR and MR, the MSLR alienated the GNR, but a complex agreement eventually led to the formation of the Cheshire Lines Committee with the MR and GNR.

Edward Watkin became the MSLR chairman for the second time in 1864, and this time he had plans to transform it from a provincial railway company into a major national player. He wanted to build a new line that would not only link his network to London, but which one day could be expanded and link to a future Channel Tunnel. It is said that Watkin prevented a merger of the three CLC partners, which would certainly have changed the course of railway history had it happened.

Watkin died in 1894, at the age of 74, having achieved most of his ambitions, if not the Channel Tunnel. His plan to extend the

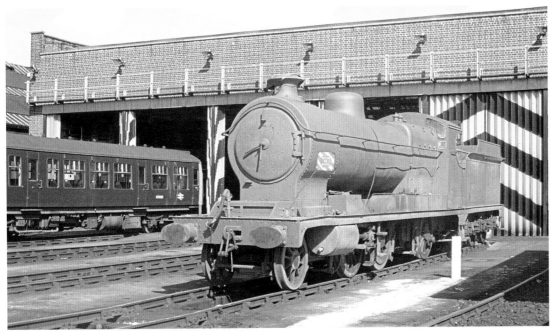

LEFT: During its long period of storage at various locations and in red oxide primer, GCR O4 2-8-0 No. 63601 is seen at Longsight shed in Manchester en route to the Dinting Railway Centre on May 18, 1976.

BELOW: No. 63601 passes Kinchley Lane on the Great Central Railway with a goods train.

MSLR to London was by then in progress, and in 1897 the company changed its name to the Great Central Railway in anticipation of the opening in 1899 of its London Extension, which proved to be the last main line railway built in Britain.

The early MSLR locomotive engineers were Richard Peacock from 1846, W G Craig from 1854, Charles R Sacre from 1859 and Thomas Parker from 1886, but Harry Pollitt took over as locomotive engineer and served through the changeover to the GCR in 1897. He was born on December 26, 1864 at Ashton-under-Lyne, the son of Sir William Pollitt, the MSLR's general manager from 1866 to 1899.

Harry Pollitt personally saw off the first GCR passenger service from Marylebone on March 15, 1899, but he resigned from the GCR in June 1900.

Two years after the appointment of John George Robinson as Pollitt's successor in 1900, the job title was changed to chief mechanical engineer. In 1872, Robinson had started an engineering apprenticeship with the GWR at Swindon works under Joseph Armstrong, and became assistant to his father, Matthew Robinson, at Bristol.

In 1884 he joined the Waterford and Limerick Railway in Ireland, and became superintendent in 1887. Robinson's locomotive designs included the 9J 'Pom'Pom' 0-6-0, which

became the LNER J11, and lasted in quantity into the 1960s; the 11E 'Director' 4-4-0 for express services from Marylebone to Sheffield and Manchester London Road; and the 8K 2-8-0, which was adopted by the Railway Operating Department for wartime service and became the LNER O4, which worked for BR right up to 1966.

He was awarded a CBE in 1920, but declined the post of chief mechanical engineer of the LNER at the Grouping, instead recommending the GNR's younger Nigel Gresley, a decision which had far-reaching consequences for British steam locomotive development.

Although we are fortunate that two of Robinson's well-known and distinctive locomotive types have survived, he was responsible for many more which are no longer with us. These include a number of Atlantic and 4-6-0 classes with charismatic names such as the 'Jersey Lily' two-cylinder simple Atlantics, the 'Fish Engine', 'Immingham' and 'Sir Sam Fay' 4-6-0s, the 8D

three-cylinder compound Atlantics, the 8H 0-6-4Ts for Wath yard, the 9N (LNER A5) Pacific tanks and the 'Faringdon' four-cylinder 4-6-0s.

O4 2-8-0 No. 63601

Robinson designed the 8K 2-8-0 for the GCR's heavy freight traffic, particularly to the new docks being built at Immingham. It was not a totally new design, but a superheated version of the 8A 0-8-0. Introduced in 1911, 126 8Ks were built before the outbreak of the First World War, and 19 more with larger boilers in 1918/21.

Strong, reliable and free-steaming, the Ministry of Munitions chose the design for its own use during the war, encouraged by the GCR's Sir Sam Fay. At this time, the Royal Engineers formed its Railway Operating Division (ROD), which started operations in Continental Europe in February 1916.

The ROD originally intended to use French and Belgian locomotives, but both of these countries deliberately kept their locomotives away from the Front, so British locomotives were quickly conscripted, and early loans included an assortment of engines from various railways. It was quickly decided that standardisation was needed, and the ROD ordered 521 of the 8K 2-8-0s in 1917/19. After the war, the ROD 2-8-0s which survived were sold to various railway companies, with the GCR itself buying three in 1919.

Thirty were sold to the LNWR and 75 to its successor the London Midland & Scottish Railway. The GWR had 100 of them, and others went to various buyers in Australia and China. Despite their success on the GCR, many of these had short lives with their new owners – the LMS ones all being scrapped or sold by the 1930s; half of the GWR fleet was gone by 1930, although others survived well into the 1950s. Thirteen locomotives were sold to J & A Brown for use on the Richmond Vale Railway in Australia.

So, the LNER inherited 131 8Ks and 17 8Ms, which became LNER O4 and O5 respectively, but all were converted to standard O4s by 1946. These were joined by no less than 273 of the former ROD locomotives between 1923 and 1927, bringing the total LNER O4 fleet to 421. However, 92 of these returned to war service when they were requisitioned by the War Department in

1941 for use in the Middle East, and none returned. Including wartime construction for the ROD and the postwar GCR 8Ms, a total of 666 locomotives were built to the GCR 2-8-0 design.

The O4s operated widely throughout the LNER system, and 58 were rebuilt by Thompson in 1944/49, with new Walschaerts valve gear, a boiler similar to a B1 4-6-0, a new cab and a raised running plate, and were classified O1. Others received only the new cab and B1 boiler, but kept the original valve gear and cylinders, becoming class O4/8. BR found itself with 329 of the LNER O4s in 1948, but five were sold to the Government in 1952 for use in Egypt, which eventually passed to the Egyptian State Railways.

Withdrawals by BR began in December 1958, and the last examples of the class were withdrawn from Doncaster in April 1966, but this was not the end of the O4s in regular service. J&A Brown operated the Richmond Vale Railway from a connection with the New South Wales Government Railways at Hexham to the Pelaw Main and Richmond Main collieries, and Australian O4 2-8-0s continued in use until 1973, while three more worked in China until 1990.

One of the GCR-built O4s – No. 63601 (originally GCR No. 102 built at Gorton in 1912) – was designated for preservation as part of the National Collection. Stored with other locomotives at Stratford works from November 1964, it moved to Leicester shed in November 1967, where it was earmarked for display in a new museum, which never materialised on the scale originally

Carrying BR lined black livery just for the last four days of its boiler certificate, GCR D11 4-4-0 No. 62660 *Butler-Henderson* departs from Loughborough Central, with a TPO train on the Great Central Railway, on February 21, 1992.

planned. It moved on to Preston Park in September 1970 then back to Leicester in August 1972, but still remained in store until loaned to the Dinting Railway Centre, where it arrived on June 20, 1976. This had once been a small GCR locomotive shed, but still no restoration work was carried out and on closure of the centre in April 1990, the O4 ended up at the National Railway Museum.

Salvation eventually came when the engine moved by road to the Great Central Railway on June 6, 1996, and restoration started at Loughborough. It returned to steam in January 2000 and became a regular, powerful and popular performer on the line, usually, rather inappropriately, in passenger service, but also frequently seen on demonstration goods trains, especially the well-known 'windcutter' rake of mineral wagons. It was withdrawn for overhaul in 2010.

Three of the 13 ROD 2-8-0s bought from the War Department by the mining firm of J&A Brown in New South Wales during the 1920s are believed to still exist. Nos. 20 & 24 (ROD Nos. 1984 & 2003) are currently owned by the Dorrigo Steam Railway, and will be a part of a planned new railway museum. No. 20 was built in 1918 by North British, and was loaned to the L&YR and LNWR during the period November 1919/August 1921, before being sold to J&A Brown in 1925. It is believed to have last steamed in 1967.

The third survivor, No. 23 (sometimes known as No. 21), was initially located at Freeman's Waterhole in New South Wales, as a part of a mining display. It has since been relocated to Richmond

Vale Railway Museum, and is understood to be undergoing a lengthy restoration process, as funds permit.

There have been moves to repatriate one of the Australian survivors to the UK, but so far without success.

11F 4-4-0 No. 506 *Butler-Henderson*

Robinson built the 11E Director 4-4-0s for the GCR in 1913, which quickly proved to be very successful, but in 1917, he built a second class of 4-6-0s, the 9P Lord Faringdons.

Although these were better than his previous 'I' class Sir Sam Fay 4-6-0s, and further ones were built, they were not an unqualified success, so five more 4-4-0s were ordered. The new 4-4-0s had a number of modifications and were classified 11F, becoming known as Improved Directors. They were delivered between 1919 and 1920, and were allocated to Neasden to haul expresses as far as Nottingham.

They proved to be even more successful than the original 11Es, and are generally acknowledged as Robinson's best express passenger design. Their 6ft 9in driving wheels made them fast, but at the same time, unsuitable for freight traffic.

A batch of six more were ordered in 1922, and by 1924 after Grouping, the LNER D10s and D11s were working from Neasden and Gorton sheds. From 1927 though, D11s were used on some of the LNER Pullman services out of King's Cross, allocated to Copley Hill in Leeds and alternating with GNR C1 Atlantics.

The LNER needed new express engines for its ex-North British routes in Scotland and decided on a batch of Improved Directors, possibly a result of Robinson's continuing influence in the new company. Twenty-four were built during 1924, modified to fit the lower NBR loading gauge. The GCR ones had been named after GCR directors, royalty, and First World War battles, but the Scottish D11/2s continued a theme set by the NBR D30 4-4-0s, and were named after characters in Sir Walter Scott's novels and poems.

By 1938, 4-6-0s were taking over and the GCR 4-4-0s were rarely seen on first-class expresses. During the early 1950s, D11s were allocated to Trafford Park and Heaton Mersey to operate the Cheshire Lines, but with regional boundary changes, were displaced by LMS types and many were put into store.

The Scottish D11/2s were spread across the NBR system, and as that railway was noted for keeping shed allocations constant, these changed little. Express passenger duties included the Scottish legs of a number of Pullman services.

They were displaced when the Gresley D49 4-4-0s arrived in Scotland in 1928, and following the advent of the Thompson B1 4-6-0s after 1945, the D11s were largely redundant, and by the 1950s, many were in storage. Nevertheless, actual withdrawals did not start until the end of 1958, but they proceeded quickly, with the last of the D11/1s going in December 1960, and the last of the D11/2s at the beginning of 1962.

The first member of the class to be built – No. 62660 *Butler Henderson* – was withdrawn by BR in 1960 – and was preserved as part of the National Collection, representing Robinson's most successful passenger design. Quickly restored to GCR condition and livery at Gorton as No. 506, it was put on display in the Museum of British Transport at Clapham, where it remained until closure in 1974.

However, it was not transferred to York with most of the other locomotive exhibits, but loaned to the Great Central Railway at

Loughborough for restoration to working order, arriving on March 14, 1975. *Butler-Henderson* returned to steam in March 1982, and brought the elegance of Robinson's finest steam locomotive design back to the line it was built for – the first time this had happened since 1960. It worked regularly for the 10 years of its boiler certificate, but on withdrawal was repainted back into GCR livery as No. 506 at Rothley and transferred to the NRM at York on April 12, 1992 for display.

In 2005 it was placed on loan to the Barrow Hill Roundhouse, not far from the now-lifted northern end of the GCR London extension, south of Sheffield.∎

ABOVE: No. 62660 *Butler-Henderson* crosses Swithland viaduct, on the Great Central Railway, on February 24, 1992, its last day in service.

BELOW: No. 506 *Butler-Henderson* on display at Barrow Hill Roundhouse.

CHAPTER 10

Metropolitan Railway

Although not part of the LNER, the Metropolitan had a joint line with the GCR and so its engines worked on LNER routes. Its goods engines were later to become LNER stock. London Transport's Metropolitan line has seen a remarkable steam revival in more recent years, even with steam through the tunnels.

ABOVE: Brill Tramway Aveling & Porter 0-4-0WT No. 807 at the Buckinghamshire Railway Centre at Quainton Road. PHIL BARNES

LEFT: Metropolitan 4-4-0T No. 23 at the Museum of British Transport at Clapham. JOHN TITLOW

This railway's first line opened in 1863, connecting Paddington, Euston and King's Cross with the City. It was the world's first underground railway.

The Met was in an unusual situation in that it was not included in the 1923 Grouping but remained independent along with other London suburban railways until the formation of London Transport in 1933. Uniquely the Met's line eventually extended as far as Verney Junction more than 50 miles from Baker Street and serving outer suburban Hertfordshire and Buckinghamshire as well as carrying freight traffic. The Met and the Great Central operated part of this route jointly. On its formation, London Transport was not interested in freight and so the outer suburban part of the Met,

BELOW: Metropolitan Railway E class 0-4-4T No. 1 in steam at Quainton Road, now known as the Buckinghamshire Railway Centre on September 15, 1985.

including its goods engines, was taken over by the LNER while its joint lines nearer London were operated by LT and the LNER.

The railway would later become the Metropolitan line of London Transport and although by then mostly electrified, steam locomotives were still used north of Rickmansworth until the early 1960s.

The former Metropolitan LNER classes M2, H2 and L2 were withdrawn before Nationalisation, having been replaced by GCR and later LNER locomotives, which were used until 1958, when the joint line was transferred to the London Midland Region and former LMS locomotives were introduced.

Two surviving Metropolitan steam locomotives were not among those taken into LNER stock, but as main line locomotives, which once ran on track owned jointly by the LNER, and in view of the close connections between the Met and the LNER it is appropriate to include them.

4-4-0T No. 23

Beyer Peacock built the A and B class condensing 4-4-0Ts for the Metropolitan Railway in 1864. They worked right across the Metropolitan system and most were withdrawn after electrification in the early 20th century.

Thirteen locomotives were retained for shunting, departmental work and working trains over the Brill Tramway from Quainton Road. The purchase of other locomotives, the closure of the Brill Tramway in 1935 and the transfer of freight working to the LNER saw all but one of these remaining locomotives sold or scrapped around 1936.

Some of the sold locomotives survived a little longer with No. 7 working on the Mersey Railway until 1939 and No. 44, which was sold to Pelaw Main Colliery in County Durham, working right up to 1948.

LT No. 45 was finally withdrawn in 1945 and was restored to Metropolitan livery as No. 23 at Neasden and occasionally exhibited to the public. It became part of the National Collection and was put on show at Clapham in 1960. The London Transport collection has moved around since the closure of Clapham in 1974 with No. 23 being kept at Syon Park and then Covent Garden.

E class 0-4-4T No. 1

Seven E class 0-4-4Ts were built for the Metropolitan Railway between 1896 and 1901, three at Neasden and four by Hawthorn Leslie.

Displaced from the main passenger trains by the H class 4-4-4T in 1920, the Es were demoted to lesser duties such as the Chesham branch, goods trains and engineers' trains.

Only four received London Transport numbers including No. 1 built at Neasden in 1898 and carrying this number because it had been a replacement for A class 4-4-0T No.1 which had been scrapped after an accident. Numbered L44 by LT, it had the honour of working the last steam-hauled LT passenger train in 1961, but continued to work engineers' trains until 1963.

L44 was saved from being broken up for scrap by the endeavours of a 19-year-old London Transport mechanical engineering apprentice called Jim Stringer, who started the Met Tank Appeal Fund in 1962. The engine originally chosen, F class 0-6-2T L52 proved to have cracked frames and L44 was the second choice offered by LT for £450. The London Railway Preservation Society, was keen to help and was assembling a collection of locomotives and stock at Luton.

A year after purchase, the London Midland Region finally granted permission for L44 to steam from Neasden to its new home at Luton, the journey taking place on Friday, March 20, 1964. The LRPS established a more permanent base at Quainton Road on the Metropolitan/GCR joint line and L44 moved here via Aylesbury in September 1970.

Restoration took a long time though and No. 1 did not return to steam until May 1985 after which it made occasional runs over a short running line with vintage coaches at what had now become the Buckinghamshire Railway Centre. Visits to other lines were rare but No. 1 did travel to the Keighley & Worth Valley Railway where it was memorably matched with the Vintage Carriages Trust's two Metropolitan coaches. It also returned to home territory to take a small part in the Steam on the Met events between 1989 and 2000, when it was withdrawn for a major overhaul.

No. 1's first trip away from home after this overhaul was to the Bluebell Railway in 2007 where it hauled the complete set of four restored Chesham branch coaches. Further trips away saw No. 1 at

Barrow Hill, Llangollen and the Mid Hants Railway.

The best was yet to come though. In 2010 an appeal was launched to fund the engine's restoration and its continued upkeep for the next 10 years to enable it to participate at many more heritage events. Following an overhaul at Bill Parker's Forest of Dean workshops, in January 2013, for the 150th Anniversary of London Underground, No. 1 made several trips between Kensington Olympia and Moorgate via Edgware Road on successive weekends to commemorate the anniversary of the first underground journey from Bishop's Road to Farringdon on January 9, 1863. The train consisted of the Bluebell's four Chesham coaches plus Metropolitan milk van No. 4 and the Metropolitan Jubilee Carriage No. 353 (the oldest-surviving operational tube carriage dating from 1892), both the property of the London Transport Museum Heritage Fleet. The operation was given added impetus by the enthusiastic support of London Mayor Boris Johnson and his Commissioner of Transport for London, Sir Peter Hendy.

No. 1 has continued to tour heritage lines as far afield as the Bodmin & Wenford Railway in Cornwall and made further underground trips on the District Line in August 2014. ∎

ABOVE: E class 0-4-4T No. 1 heads the Bluebell Railway's four restored Metropolitan Chesham branch coaches at Horsted Keynes in August 2007.

BELOW: No. 1 heads a Metropolitan 150th anniversary train through Paddington Circle Line station on January 13, 2013.
JOHN TITLOW

CHAPTER 11

Great North of Scotland Railway

Although one of the smallest constituent companies of the LNER, this railway is surprisingly well represented in the heritage era.

ABOVE: GNSR F class 4-4-0 No. 49 *Gordon Highlander* at Turriff on the GNSR branch to Macduff on June 13, 1960.
TB OWEN / COLOUR-RAIL.COM

The GNSR was one of the smaller Scottish railways, operating in the far north-east of the country. Formed in 1845, it carried its first passengers the 39 miles from Kittybrewster to Huntly on September 20, 1854.

By 1867 it had grown to 226¼ route miles, and by the 1880s operated a main line between Aberdeen and Keith and two routes west to Elgin, connecting with Highland Railway services to Inverness. Branches served the fishing ports on the north coast and the GNSR took over the Deeside branch from Aberdeen to Ballater.

Fish from the North Sea and whisky from Speyside were important goods traffic and the royal family used the Deeside Line for travel to and from Balmoral. The railway's first locomotives were 2-4-0s, built by Wm Fairbairn in Manchester to the design of the locomotive superintendent Daniel Kinnear Clark. The railway opened with only five locomotives, and within days one had been seriously damaged in a collision and a second had a mechanical fault.

John Folds Ruthven replaced Clark in 1855 and after William Cowan became locomotive superintendent, nine more locomotives arrived in 1859-61. These were followed by nine 4-4-0s, built by Robert Stephenson & Co and delivered in 1862-64, after which time the GNSR came to be operated very largely by 4-4-0s.

After James Manson became locomotive superintendent in 1883 more modern locomotives were introduced but in 1890 Manson was replaced by James Johnson, the son of Samuel W Johnson, then locomotive superintendent of the Midland Railway. In 1893 Neilson's delivered six more-powerful 4-4-0s which set the standard for the GNSR's later locomotive development.

William Pickersgill replaced Johnson in 1894, and 26 4-4-0s were purchased from Neilson's, similar to Johnson's S class. Pickersgill moved the company's locomotive works from Kittybrewster to Inverurie before

Thomas E Heywood took over in 1914, and after the war, six more locomotives were built by North British and two at Inverurie. Similar to the 1899 locomotives but with Robinson superheaters, these were given names. Heywood also changed the livery during the war, the traditional green being replaced by black lined with yellow and red.

In 1923, the GNSR became part of the LNER passing on 333½ miles of line and 122 steam locomotives, most of them 4-4-0s. It was isolated from the rest of the LNER as the NBR had used running rights over the Caledonian to reach Aberdeen. The GNSR's only remaining main line today is the eastern part of the Aberdeen to Inverness line as far as Keith. Forty-four of its locomotives lasted until 1948 and the last two GNSR locomotives to be withdrawn were two of the Aberdeen harbour 0-4-2Ts in 1960. Heritage lines established on one-time GNSR routes are the 11-mile Keith and Dufftown Railway and the relatively new Royal Deeside Railway at Milton of Crathes.

F class 4-4-0 No. 49 *Gordon Highlander*

In February 1898, Neilson Reid had completed an order for 12 4-4-0s for the GNSR, which the railway designated T class, and in October that year, Pickersgill, the locomotive superintendent, requested authority to purchase a further 12. Neilson Reid offered to build between 10 and 20 to the T class design, but the GNSR board granted permission for only 10 slightly modified locomotives, designated V class. The first was delivered in October 1899, but by the time the first five had been received, a downturn in traffic meant that not only were the remaining five not required, the railway could not afford them anyway. Fortunately, at the GNSR's request, the builders sold them to the South Eastern & Chatham which would have bought the first five as well if the GNSR had been prepared to sell. A further eight were later built by the GNSR at its Inverurie works, in 1909-10.

KEITH + DUFFTOWN RAILWAY

ABERDEEN

MALLAIG

ROYAL DEESIDE RAILWAY

FORT WILLIAM

DUNDEE

PERTH

GLASGOW

BO'NESS & KINNEIL RAILWAY

EDINBURGH

BERWICK

ALN VALLEY RAILWAY

NEWCASTLE

SUNDERLAND

CARLISLE

TANFIELD RAILWAY

The GNSR F class introduced in 1920 by TE Heywood was simply a superheated V class, and members were the only ones to be named by the GNSR. The class comprised eight locomotives, six built by North British in Glasgow in 1920, and the remaining two by the railway at Inverurie in 1921. They represented the final development of the GNSR 4-4-0 which was first introduced in 1862, and always formed the mainstay of the line's services.

All 21 GNSR V and F class 4-4-0s were inherited by the LNER in 1923, which classed both superheated and non-superheated ones as D40.

The GNSR used the Vs and Fs for the most important express services as they were the last 4-4-0s built by the GNSR, which unlike other companies never introduced larger Atlantics or 4-6-0s. They usually worked the line from Aberdeen to Keith and Elgin, although they were sometimes used on through workings to Inverness via the Highland Railway. Although the newer 4-4-0s were the GNSR's best express locomotives, they also had to take their turn on goods and branch line workings alongside the older GNSR 4-4-0s.

The D40s continued these express passenger duties after Grouping, but they were joined by ex-NBR D31 4-4-0s in 1925 and in 1931 were finally displaced from the heaviest passenger services by transfers of B12 4-6-0s from East Anglia.

The D40s were increasingly relegated to branch line duties and the first one was withdrawn in 1947, but 18 passed into BR ownership in 1948. At this time, large numbers of Thompson B1 4-6-0s were being introduced, and BR quickly withdrew the remaining 18 D40s between February 1953 and June 1958. The last D40 in service was No. 62277 *Gordon Highlander* which was withdrawn in 1958 from Kittybrewster shed at Aberdeen.

No. 62277 was preserved by BR as an example of the superheated version and restored to GNSR condition as No. 49. It was turned out in GNSR green although it never carried green livery in GNSR service since it originally appeared in Heywood's lined

black. Restored to working order, it was soon put to work in 1959 along with other Scottish preserved engines double heading specials to a trade fair in Aberdeen, after which it remained available for railtour and excursion service, normally based at Dawsholm shed in Glasgow.

It was occasionally seen on timetabled services on GNSR routes but retired again in October 1964 and after a period of storage at Parkhead shed was put on display in the new Glasgow Transport Museum originally at Pollokshields in June 1966. It has, however, recently been moved to the Scottish Railway Museum at Bo'ness rather than the new harbourside Glasgow Transport Museum. ■

ABOVE: No. 49 in the Scottish Railway Museum at Bo'ness. ROBIN JONES

CHAPTER 12

NBR C class 0-6-0
No. 673 *Maude* climbs away
from Glenfinnan viaduct on
the West Highland extension
to Mallaig on May 28, 1984

North British Railway

The most important of the LNER's Scottish constituents, the NBR, worked the Scottish part of the East Coast Main Line to Edinburgh, and on over the Forth Bridge. Its West Highland line now sees regular steam action.

The NBR was established in 1844 and its original Edinburgh to Berwick-upon-Tweed line was completed in 1846, forming the northernmost part of the East Coast Main Line from 1848. The fastest trains between the two capitals then took slightly over 12½ hours by either the East Coast or West Coast routes, but the cheaper steamship service between Leith and London still carried most of the passenger traffic.

The first major extension of the system was a branch to Hawick in 1849, extended by the Border Union Railway to give a through route to the WCML at Carlisle in 1862, which became the NBR's Waverley route. From the Waverley Route, a branch to Hexham, connecting with the NER's Newcastle-Carlisle line, gave the NBR running rights into Newcastle which it never had from Berwick.

The NBR grew to have about 450 miles of route by 1865. Mineral traffic (in particular coal from the Lothian coalfield) was the largest source of revenue. Although primarily a Scottish railway, the NBR also had an extensive branch network in northern Northumberland, reaching Hexham, Morpeth and Rothbury, as well as the main line into Berwick.

The NBR operated services between Edinburgh Waverley and Glasgow Queen Street and was a partner with the NER and GNR in the East Coast Joint Stock operation from 1860.

The Edinburgh, Perth and Dundee Railway, serving Fife, was absorbed into the NBR in 1862. Its service from Edinburgh to Dundee was more direct than the Caledonian route via Stirling and Perth, but involved ferry crossings of both the Firth of Forth and the Firth of Tay, removing much of its competitive advantage for both passenger and goods traffic.

The Tay Bridge opened in 1878 but collapsed in a high wind on December 28, 1879, bringing disgrace on its designer Sir Thomas Bouch. Questions raised by this and the time building a replacement which opened in 1887 caused delays in finally bridging the Forth.

The 8296ft Forth Bridge was opened on March 4, 1890, having taken seven years to build. It was proposed by the NBR but was built and owned jointly with the Midland, Great Northern and North Eastern railways, which all ran services over NBR tracks. On Grouping, the Forth Bridge became joint LNER and LMS property.

Construction of the West Highland Railway from Glasgow to Fort William was authorised in 1889, with work starting in October. The line was opened on August 7, 1894, and extended to Mallaig by the Mallaig Extension Railway on April 1, 1901. The West Highland Railway was absorbed by the NBR on December 21, 1908, becoming a major and well-known part of the system.

The NBR's first locomotive superintendent, from 1867-1874, was Thomas Wheatley, born in Micklefield, Leeds, in 1821. Better known though was Dugald Drummond (January 1, 1840 – November 8, 1912), who had worked for the London Brighton & South Coast Railway and later held the position of locomotive superintendent with the Caledonian Railway and later London and South Western Railway.

Matthew Holmes from Paisley (1844-1903) was the chief mechanical engineer of the NBR from 1882 to 1903, whose locomotive designs include the C class 0-6-0, later LNER J36, and the M class 4-4-0 (LNER D31).

William Paton Reid (1854 –1932) was apprenticed to the NBR's Cowlairs works in 1879 and was locomotive superintendent from 1903 to 1919. Reid modernised and rebuilt existing engines and introduced superheating to the NBR. He was also responsible for several long-lived designs, particularly 4-4-0s and 0-6-0s, including what became the LNER D34 and J37. Reid introduced a class of Atlantics which were never totally successful and after they were withdrawn in 1937 there was a plan to preserve No. 9875 and it re-entered service for a while. However, it was withdrawn for repairs in November 1939 and was scrapped during the Second World War.

Walter Chalmers was the NBR's last CME but having taken up his post in 1920 had little opportunity to make his mark, although he did design a three-cylinder 2-8-0 for coal traffic which never got beyond

the drawing board. In 1923 the NBR was the largest railway company in Scotland, and the fifth largest in the UK.

The main heritage line running on former NBR trackage is the Bo'ness & Kinneil Railway, which grew from the Scottish Railway Preservation Society, owner of the preserved C class (J36) 0-6-0 No. 673 *Maude*. The only other NBR survivors are the 4-4-0 No. 256 *Glen Douglas* in the National Collection and 0-4-0ST No. 42.

G class 0-4-0ST No. 42

The G class was a class of 0-4-0ST shunter introduced in 1882, some of which were equipped with small wooden tenders to carry extra coal; 38 entered service on the NBR between 1882 and 1899. The design was originated by Neilson and Co of Hyde Park Works, Springburn, Glasgow, which had built the first examples of the type in the 1870s.

In 1876 the Caledonian Railway had bought four, then built 34 more itself. The NBR bought two from Neilson and built another 36. Both main line railways credited their own CMEs with the design. The LNER acquired most of the NBR ones in 1923 and classified them Y9, and 33 of them passed into BR ownership in 1948.

No. 68095 worked in Leith docks and was the last to be withdrawn, in December 1962. It was bought from BR straight out of traffic at St Margaret's shed, Edinburgh, by Jim Morris, and after a period of storage at Shettleston was displayed at his small museum at Lytham St Annes in Lancashire from December 1966. The museum closed and the engine was bought by the Scottish Railway Preservation Society with the aid of a grant from the National Fund for Acquisitions, arriving at Bo'ness on February 16, 1992.

The NBR painted its goods engines black, but the engine is displayed in the Scottish Railway Museum as No. 42 in NBR bronze green passenger livery. It has never steamed in preservation.

ABOVE: NBR G class 0-4-0ST No. 42 on display in the Scottish Railway Museum at Bo'ness.

TOP: The three NBR survivors, Nos. 42, 65243 *Maude* and 256 *Glen Douglas* line up at Bo'ness.
IAN LOTHIAN

TOP: No. 673 *Maude* heads through Drumlanrigg gorge on the Glasgow & South Western main line on May 17, 1980.

BELOW: No. 673 crosses Ais Gill viaduct on the Settle & Carlisle line.

C class 0-6-0 No. 673 *Maude*

Matthew Holmes designed the C class 0-6-0 for NBR goods traffic. They were introduced in 1888 and a total of 168 locomotives was built, 138 by the NBR at Cowlairs while the other 30 were split equally between Neilson and Sharp Stewart.

They were needed largely as a result of the opening of the second Tay Bridge in July 1887 and the imminent opening of the Forth Bridge in March 1890, which was expected to generate considerable extra traffic.

The Cs could be found all over the NBR system, and although initially used for long distance goods work, even by 1900 they were being regularly used on passenger duties. They were displaced by the larger superheated S class (LNER J37) 0-6-0s from 1918 when many Cs were moved to local mineral,

trip pilot and banking duties in place of older 0-6-0s.

During the First World War, 25 of the class were sent to France for service with the Railway Operating Division and on their return to Scotland they were given names of battles, generals and even a cartoon soldier in recognition of their service. The names were hand-painted on the splasher above the middle driving wheel so often disappeared during repaints, especially on visits to 'foreign' works.

All 168 passed into the hands of the LNER in 1923 and became class J36. Withdrawals started in 1931 but paused during the Second World War; 123 were inherited by BR in 1948 and many were reallocated to ex-GNSR sheds and ex-LMS sheds in Scotland. The last J36s proved particularly long-lived and outlasted not only larger 0-6-0s but also much later LNER designs and BR Standards. Six were still at work in May 1966, and when the last two, No. 65288 of Dunfermline (62C) and No. 65345 of Thornton Junction (62A), were finally withdrawn on June 5, 1967, they were the last main line steam locomotives in service in Scotland.

C class No. 673 was rebuilt at Cowlairs in 1915 and was one of those sent to support the army in France. After its return to Scotland in 1919, No. 673 was named *Maude* after Lieutenant General Sir Fredrick Stanley Maude, who had commanded the successful British forces in Mesopotamia until his death from cholera in 1917.

Maude was withdrawn from Bathgate as No. 65243 in 1966, and after a successful fundraising appeal by the Scottish Railway Preservation Society, it was purchased for preservation and moved to the SRPS base at Falkirk on January 19, 1967. It was restored to working order, painted in NBR lined black goods livery as No. 673 , returning to steam in September 1978. The SRPS had still not found itself a length of line to run on and, remarkably, *Maude* obtained a main line certificate and embarked on a railtour programme which even took it to the West Highland line in 1984. It also made it to Inverness with a couple of coaches and made the epic journey via the Glasgow & South Western and the Settle & Carlisle to Rainhill on Merseyside with two Caledonian coaches from the SRPS collection for the Liverpool & Manchester Rocket 150 cavalcade in May 1980.

Having finally settled on the Bo'ness branch as its length of operating railway, the SRPS moved all its stock to Bo'ness and No. 673 made the move on January 10, 1988. Its working future would be on the Bo'ness & Kinneil Railway. It made a return to BR livery in 1996 for a short period but is now under overhaul.

K class 4-4-0 No. 256 *Glen Douglas*

The K class covered four types of NBR 4-4-0 which originated with a Matthew Holmes express design in 1902. Reid's three varieties of 6ft driving wheel 4-4-0 were basically mixed traffic variants, starting with the Scotts, then Superheated Scotts and finally the Glens. The first 10 of the latter were built in 1913 at Cowlairs and three later batches totalling 20 were built between 1917 and 1920. Reid's 4-4-0s were popular and versatile and the K class carried the names of various Scottish glens. They were later classified D34 by the LNER.

Three-quarters of the class was initially allocated to Eastfield, and used extensively on the West Highland line, duties which continued until Nationalisation, although limited to 190-ton trains on the route, requiring frequent doubleheading. Despite the introduction of much more powerful classes as early as 1927, the D34s continued to be associated with the line until their withdrawal.

The LNER kept over half of its D34s allocated to Eastfield, with the remainder usually allocated to Thornton Junction or Edinburgh St Margarets; their duties including passenger services from Glasgow to Edinburgh via Polmont and Glasgow to Thornton and Dundee. The St Margarets D34s also worked alongside the D32s and D33s on passenger services to Berwick, Hawick and Galashiels.

Although the first Glen was withdrawn in 1946 as Thompson B1 4-6-0s came on stream, it was not until 1958 that withdrawals started in earnest, and all were withdrawn by 1961. No. 62469 *Glen Douglas* was painted into NBR livery as No. 256 in 1959 and put to work along with other Scottish preserved engines doubleheading specials to a trade fair in Aberdeen. It was not actually withdrawn from regular service until 1961 and was used on railtours, based at Dawsholm, until finally retired in 1964.

On June 1, 1963, it doubleheaded with a J37 0-6-0 on the last steam passenger train over the West Highland line from Glasgow to Fort William and Mallaig. Unfortunately both had failed by Fort William with hot axleboxes as did both substitute J37s, and the train returned from Mallaig to Glasgow diesel-hauled.

After a period of storage at Parkhead shed, it was put on display in the new Glasgow Transport Museum at Kelvinhall in June 1966, but was moved to the Scottish Railway Museum at Bo'ness in February 1992 with the possibility of a return to steam. Financial support was never forthcoming however and it was moved to the new waterfront Glasgow Transport Museum. ∎

In BR black livery, No. 65243 *Maude* heads a photo charter goods train at Bo'ness in November 1996. GEOFF SILCOCK

No. 256 *Glen Douglas* and J37 0-6-0 No. 64632 pause at Garelochhead with the Scottish Locomotive Preservation Fund's 'Jacobite' from Glasgow to Mallaig on June 1 1963. GAVIN MORRISON

CHAPTER 13

London & North Eastern Railway

One of the 'Big Four' companies created in 1923, the LNER built on the successes of its already highly rated constituents.

On the 50th anniversary of the closure of the Midland & Great Northern Joint Railway system in February 2009, GER N7 0-6-2T No. 69621 approaches Weybourne on the North Norfolk Railway, passing LNER B1 4-6-0 No. 1306 *Mayflower*.

Formed on January 1, 1923, by the amalgamation mainly of the GNR, NER, GER, GCR, NBR and GNSR, the LNER's territory centred on the East Coast Main Line from King's Cross to Edinburgh and on to Kinnaber Junction, north of Montrose. East of this was exclusively LNER territory, while the former GCR routes penetrated well to the west, to Banbury, Derby and Liverpool. The NER ran to the west coast, to Carlisle, and in Scotland the situation was particularly confused with the NBR having lines to Carlisle and to Fort William and Mallaig, while the line from Kinnaber Junction into Aberdeen, being formerly Caledonian, was now LMS.

There were many joint lines, the Cheshire Lines Committee becoming joint LNER/LMS property, but the Midland & Great Northern Joint did not, remaining independent until 1936, when the LNER took it over.

The formation of British Railways initially saw the LNER split into the Eastern, North Eastern and part of the Scottish Region, this causing quite a lot of confusion which was gradually corrected.

The Scottish Region was simple; all LMS and LNER routes north of the border were amalgamated with only very minor exceptions such as NBR routes south of the border.

The North Eastern Region was basically the North Eastern Railway while the Eastern Region consisted of GNR, GER and GCR routes. This led to a large amount of overlap, particularly in the West Riding, not just of ER and NER territory but overlapping with LMS routes as well. Eventually a geographical border was established to the north of Sheffield and Doncaster, north of which was NER regardless of pre-Grouping origin, with the LNER/LMSR border being the border between Lancashire and Yorkshire. LMSR (mainly Midland) routes around Sheffield

all became Eastern Region with a geographical border established west of Sheffield and Chesterfield. Other minor tweaking took place to avoid overlapping lines in the East Midlands.

The map of the former LNER has inevitably retracted, the major closures having been the M&GN in 1959, much of the GCR, many GNR routes in Lincolnshire and GER routes in East Anglia, the NER Harrogate – Thirsk, Wensleydale and Stainmore routes and the NBR's Waverley route from Edinburgh to Carlisle and associated branches. The NER also lost three out of the four routes to Whitby.

In the preservation era, three major heritage lines on former LNER routes where LNER engines can usually be seen are the North Yorkshire Moors Railway, the Great Central Railway and the North Norfolk Railway.

At the Grouping, John Robinson of the GCR was offered the position of CME of the newly formed LNER, but the elderly Robinson declined and suggested the much younger Herbert Nigel Gresley from the GNR. Robinson had a more established track record of locomotive design but Gresley had just made a name for himself with his first A1 Pacifics, which were clearly seen as the way forward.

Gresley was an innovator and while he produced some of the most powerful and charismatic conventional steam locomotives ever to run in Britain, he experimented with unconventional designs as well, with varying degrees of success. His huge P1 2-8-2s could haul coal trains so long that the loops and sidings could not accommodate them, the marine water-tube boilered W1 'hush-hush' 4-6-4 No. 10000 was a bit of a disaster and the relatively unusual P2 2-8-2s for the Aberdeen road, while powerful, were unpopular and uneconomic in service.

LNER A4 Pacific No. 60009 *Union of South Africa* departs from Goathland on the North Yorkshire Moors Railway and passes NER Q6 0-8-0 No. 63395 with a northbound goods train.

During the 1930s, Nigel Gresley lived at Salisbury Hall near St Albans, and in 1936 he was awarded an honorary DSc by Manchester University and a knighthood by King Edward VIII.

He was the designer of some of the most famous steam locomotives in Britain, including the A1 and the streamlined A4 Pacifics. In 1934, A1 Pacific No. 4472 *Flying Scotsman* was the first steam locomotive officially recorded over 100mph, and in 1938 a streamlined A4, No. 4468 *Mallard*, captured the record for being the fastest steam locomotive in the world at 126mph, which has never been beaten.

Gresley looked at modern traction for his high-speed services from King's Cross to Leeds, Newcastle and Edinburgh and decided against it, but in 1936 he was involved in designing the 1500V DC electric locomotives for the proposed electrification of the Woodhead route between Manchester and Sheffield. The Second World War forced the postponement of the project, which was completed in the early 1950s.

Gresley was a prolific locomotive designer and we have several high-profile Gresley products gracing heritage lines and the main lines, notably A3 and A4 Pacifics, V2 2-6-2, K4 2-6-0, D49 4-4-0 and N2 0-6-2T. Many of his equally well-known classes are extinct though, including the K2 and K3 moguls, O2 2-8-0, B17 Sandringham 4-6-0 and his most numerous class, the J39 0-6-0. The more unorthodox Gresley designs such as the U1 2-8-2-2-8-2 Garratt and the water-tube boilered W1 4-6-4 No. 10000 were scrapped or rebuilt too early to have stood a chance of preservation.

Gresley died after a short illness on April 5, 1941, and was buried in Netherseal, Derbyshire. He was succeeded by Edward Thompson as the LNER CME .

LOCOMOTIVE LIVERY

The GNR had standardised on apple green within a darker green panel and brown frames. The NER had a slightly lighter shade of green while the GCR had mid-green and dark red frames. The GER adopted ultramarine blue, the NBR bronze green and the GNSR light green. However there was increasing use of black or grey liveries during the First World War and after 1918 GNSR engines remained black and GER engines grey.

For the LNER's express engines, Gresley standardised on apple green, with black and white lining and black frames with red lining. Lettering was gold leaf shaded red, black and white. Goods engines were plain black with red and yellow lettering and passenger engines had the addition of red lining.

Apple green was interpreted somewhat differently by different locomotive works, particularly by Darlington. While Doncaster and Stratford stuck with black cylinder covers, Darlington always preferred green.

The only variations to these liveries were the first four A4 Pacifics which were initially turned out in two-tone grey, followed by some in garter blue with dark red wheels. No.10000 also carried the silver livery. Thompson painted his A1 No. 4470 *Great Northern* rebuild in dark blue but simplified the standard apple green locomotive livery by replacing the shaded lettering with plain yellow.

During the First World War, plain matt black was standard, but after the war, the A4s regained their garter blue livery but now with stainless steel lettering. BR applied its standard locomotive liveries to all LNER engines and the Class 8 Pacifics carried blue livery for a while before all gained Brunswick green colours after 1950. The only variations were the J72 and J69 0-6-0Ts used as Newcastle, York and Liverpool Street station pilots, which briefly carried NER green and GER blue liveries respectively around 1960. The Doncaster/Darlington livery variations were perpetuated in BR days with Darlington lining out the cylinder covers while Doncaster did not.

In preservation, virtually all preserved LNER engines quickly reverted to LNER colours with the notable exception of A4 Pacific No. 60009 *Union of South Africa* which has carried BR livery throughout. Many enthusiasts regretted the fact that preserved LNER engines looked nothing like the ones they remembered but it was only in the 1990s that LNER engines started to be seen in BR livery carrying the familiar five-digit numbers beginning with '6'.

There has been a move recently back to apple green or pre-Grouping liveries but surprisingly no LNER passenger tender engine has yet been seen in preservation in lined out LNER black livery.

LNER A3 Pacific No. 4472 *Flying Scotsman* at York station with its first 'Scarborough Spa Express' since purchase by the NRM in 2004.

TOP LEFT: During its USA tour, *Flying Scotsman* is seen at Boston, Massachusetts.

TOP RIGHT: No. 4472 arrives at Market Overton in October 1973. DAVID FORD

BELOW: On one of its 60th anniversary runs over the ECML from Peterborough, LNER A3 Pacific No. 4472 *Flying Scotsman* departs from Doncaster on March 6, 1983.

A3 4-6-2 No. 4472 *Flying Scotsman*

Britain's first Pacific was the Great Western Railway's *The Great Bear,* designed by Churchward in 1908, but no more were built and it was not until 1922 that Raven built Pacifics for the NER and Gresley started building some for the GNR.

A third of Gresley's GNR Pacifics did not emerge from Doncaster until after Grouping and became a member of the LNER's A1 class. Although the GNR named the first Pacific *Great Northern,* it was the LNER's decision to exhibit No. 4472 at the British Empire Exhibition in 1924 which led to it being named *Flying Scotsman,* the name by which the 10am departure from King's Cross to Edinburgh was unofficially known.

The engine's next claim to fame was being chosen to head the first non-stop run of the 'Flying Scotsman' from King's Cross to Edinburgh in May 1928, and of course there has been confusion between the locomotive and the train ever since, the train having been officially designated in 1927.

Although never regarded as the best of the A1s, No. 4472 received another great honour in 1934 when it became the first steam engine in Britain to be officially recorded as travelling at 100mph.

By then the A1 design had been enhanced and new Gresley Pacifics were being built as A3s, with the older ones being progressively rebuilt. *Flying Scotsman* was one of the last A1s to remain in its original condition and was probably lucky not to have been rebuilt by Thompson; a fate which befell sister engine and class pioneer No. 4470 *Great Northern.*

Flying Scotsman was rebuilt to A3 specification in 1949 and became BR's No. 60103; by now the A3s were playing second fiddle to the streamlined A4 Pacifics and Peppercorn's A1s were coming on stream. Nevertheless, very late in its life, along with most A3s, No. 60103 was given the benefit of a double chimney which transformed its performance if only for the last few months of its working life.

It is hard to imagine a steam engine having a better pedigree than that of *Flying Scotsman;* yet it was not selected for official preservation by the British Transport Commission. *Mallard* clearly had the edge and there just was not room on the list for two Gresley Pacifics. No. 60103 was also considered so far removed now from the original Gresley A1 design as to not qualify on that basis either.

However, Retford businessman Alan Pegler had brought the two Ivatt Atlantics out of York museum and run them from King's Cross

in 1952; he had bought the Ffestiniog Railway in 1955, and now, on the BR Eastern Region board, buying a Gresley Pacific and running it on the main line would appear to be a piece of cake.

No. 60103 set off from King's Cross on its last run in BR service, the 1pm to Leeds, on January 14, 1963. It left the train at Doncaster, went into the works and emerged in April in Alan Pegler's ownership, with single chimney reinstated and in LNER apple green livery carrying the number 4472. Alan had been to the British Empire Exhibition in 1924 and was so impressed with the engine that when he had the opportunity to buy it 40 years later he could not resist.

Pegler had bought it to run it, negotiating a contract with BR for its continued operation until 1972, a contract no one else managed to obtain. Starting with a run from Paddington to Ruabon for the Ffestiniog Railway, No. 4472 gradually penetrated many unfamiliar parts of the BR system, this being made easier from 1966 after the purchase of a second tender.

From October 1967, *Flying Scotsman* became the only privately owned steam engine able to run on BR and from August 1968 and the end of BR steam, it was Britain's only main line steam engine. Yet rather than capitalise on this monopoly situation, Pegler took his engine to the United States in 1969 for a promotional tour, an attraction being that he could drive his own engine. After a successful tour, another tour was embarked on but this one proved disastrous. Pegler went bankrupt, the engine was seized by creditors and was left stranded in America. Maybe the only preserved non-streamlined Gresley Pacific would be lost after all. A rescue operation was masterminded by long-time *Scotsman* minder George Hinchcliffe, bankrolled by William

McAlpine. No. 4472 was soon on a ship heading east across the Atlantic, arriving in Liverpool in February 1972. Amazingly, after braving the Atlantic storms on the deck of the vessel, the A3 was pronounced fit to travel under its own steam to Derby works for overhaul.

It had returned to a very different railway system to the one it had left three years earlier, but there were now heritage lines which could run a Class 8 express engine. Consequently, No. 4472's first assignment was a summer season working on the one-time GWR Torbay Steam Railway where it arrived on July 15, 1973. Its triumphant return to main line passenger duties saw it doubleheading with GWR 4-6-0 No. 6000 *King George V* on the Welsh Marches route in September after which it adjourned to its new home at Market Overton in Rutland that November.

The scheme for a heritage line and main line base in Rutland came to nothing and McAlpine instead got involved with the leading centre for main line steam, Steamtown at Carnforth, Lancashire, where *Flying Scotsman* moved to on August 11, 1974, arriving at the head of an overnight empty stock train from Kensington Olympia. This in itself was an indication that the A3 and particularly its owner would not always be subject to the strict interpretation of BR's new rules relating to steam operation.

A busy 10 years saw the engine working railtours in most parts of the country but the return of regular steam to the London area saw *Scotsman* relocated to Marylebone for working upmarket dining trains to Stratford-upon-Avon in December 1985; however, its base changed to Southall on February 27, 1988, where better facilities existed for an extensive overhaul to prepare the engine for its greatest adventure yet.

TOP LEFT: No. 4472 has just departed from Marylebone on October 26, 1986 and emerges from Lords tunnel, crossing over the West Coast Main Line at South Hampstead.

TOP RIGHT: *Flying Scotsman* **passes Neasden on the GC/GW joint line from High Wycombe on January 3, 1987.**

BELOW*: Flying Scotsman* **heads its first passenger working of its Australian tour, from Melbourne to Albury, past Broadford, on October 25, 1988.**

Flying Scotsman travelled to Australia to be the star attraction at the Aus Steam 88 festival in Melbourne in October 1988, part of the country's bicentennial celebrations. It spent most of the time on display but was allowed out for a couple of main line excursions, even taking part in a triple parallel run.

In 1989, *Scotsman* was more adventurous and journeyed not only right across the Nullarbor Plain to Perth where it was reunited with GWR 4-6-0 No. 4079 *Pendennis Castle*, but also through the red heart of Australia to Alice Springs, probably two of the most hostile environments in which to attempt to operate a steam engine.

On its return from Australia, No. 4472 quickly returned to its former duties, still nominally based at Southall, but it was proving to be a drain on even Lord McAlpine's pocket, and a half share in Flying Scotsman Railways, which owned Steamtown, *Flying Scotsman* and much more besides, was sold to Pete Waterman. The main effect of this was that the engine gained a double

chimney, emerging from an overhaul at Babcock Robey Engineering in BR Brunswick green livery with a double chimney and carrying the number 60103. It again went straight into a summer season on what was now the Paignton & Dartmouth Steam Railway in 1993 but did not have a main line certificate.

It spent a few years pottering around mainly ex-GWR heritage lines in deteriorating mechanical condition. Waterman's venture into main line steam operations foundered somewhat in the uncertain brave new world of railway privatisation and the joint owners wanted out. *Flying Scotsman* was purchased by nouveau riche entrepreneur, the late Tony Marchington, who contracted the engine's long-time engineer, Roland Kennington, to carry out possibly the most extensive and expensive rebuild of any preserved steam engine in Britain.

It was a close-run thing and the paint was still wet when renumbered No. 4472 steamed out of King's Cross at the head of

No. 4472 *Flying Scotsman* passes the flat crossing at Newark on July 11, 1999, on its second working in the ownership of Tony Marchington. ROBIN STEWART-SMITH

Marchington's first upmarket steam dining excursion in July 1999, the engine's first visit to its one-time home territory for 30 years. It had hauled its last excursion in Alan Pegler's ownership out of King's Cross on August 31, 1969, immediately before the disastrous American trip. Steam had then been banned from the terminus until after Privatisation in 1994, and this was *Scotsman's* first chance to return to its home turf.

All went well and thousands lined the route just like the old days, but enthusiasts were horrified. The A3 still had its double chimney but was back in LNER apple green as No. 4472. What was possibly worse was that the A3 had an A4 boiler and rebored cylinders in a bid to produce sufficient power to haul rather longer trains up rather steeper hills than Gresley had envisaged in 1922.

Marchington's own excursions faded away and enthusiasts' railtours with *Scotsman* were rare, but the engine was signed up for the Venice Simplon Orient-Express Pullman workings mainly on the Southern Region. These were very heavy trains. Opinion is divided as to whether *Scotsman* was now simply exerting more power than the basic structure of the engine could cope with on a regular basis or not; but the finances of Flying Scotsman plc became more and more stretched and keeping the engine running proved increasingly difficult.

Eventually, among ever more wild rumours, the engine was offered for sale by auction and a phenomenally successful fundraising campaign by the National Railway Museum saw it secured for the nation in 2004, 41 years too late in many people's opinion. Arriving at York complete with main line certificate, No. 4472's record of reliability running for its new owners was poor. It was withdrawn for overhaul, the circumstances of which and the costs incurred proving to be even more controversial. Against a background of mutual recriminations over just what state the engine was in when purchased, the engine has been stripped down, rebuilt, then dismantled again twice so far and an 18-month project looks likely to take 10 years and cost three times the original estimate. *Flying Scotsman* is no longer the most famous steam locomotive in the world, as in the meantime, a new Peppercorn A1 Pacific called *Tornado* has been built and has stolen *Scotsman's* crown.

The hope is, of course, that *Flying Scotsman* will emerge from its overhaul in 2015 and regain its rightful position as the world's favourite steam engine. It certainly has a history like no other.

No. 4472 departs from Scarborough for York with its first 'Scarborough Spa Express' since purchase by the NRM in 2004.

Flying Scotsman **passes Loughborough Midland with a Christmas dining train from Tyseley just before withdrawal for overhaul at the NRM in December 2005.**

LNER B12 4-6-0 No. 61572 passes Greenwood on the ECML with the M&GNJRS 'Wandering 1500' from Broad Street to Stratford-upon-Avon on October 5, 1963. COLOUR-RAIL.COM

Finally returned to steam, LNER B12 4-6-0 No. 8572 climbs towards Kelling Heath on March 4, 1995 on the North Norfolk Railway.

B12/3 4-6-0 No. 8572

The GER S69, or 1500 class 4-6-0, was originally designed by Stephen Holden but much rebuilt, resulting in several subclasses. 71 were built between 1911 and 1921 and a further 10 locomotives were built by Beyer Peacock in 1928.

They were designed to replace the Claud Hamilton 4-4-0s on GE express services, but producing a more powerful engine was difficult because of the design constraints of axle loading and short turntables, resulting in a very short 4-6-0; an unusual design but nevertheless a very versatile locomotive. The large cab resulted in an 8ft distance between the firebox door and the tender, requiring the fireman to use a long-handled shovel.

They eventually took over all of the GER express services from London including the Cambridge services. After Grouping, Gresley had ideas for a three-cylinder 4-6-0 design but the GE section could not wait and the final batch of 10 B12s was ordered. Classified B12/2, these differed from the originals with the addition of Lentz poppet valve gear and no decorative framing over the driving wheels.

The LNER also wanted B12s for the Great North of Scotland lines but the GE's shortage was critical and transfers to Scotland did not take place until 1931 after Gresley's B17 4-6-0s had taken over GE line expresses. Over the next 10 years, 31 B12s moved to Scotland, initially for passenger services between Elgin and Aberdeen, but later elsewhere.

Between 1932 and 1944, all ten B12/2s and 44 of the original B12/1s were rebuilt with long-travel Stephenson piston valves and larger boilers with round-topped fireboxes. They were classified B12/3, but none of the GNS engines received new boilers. However, nine more B12/1s were given new boilers in 1943 and classified B12/4, being allocated to low axle load lines in Scotland. In view of the extensive rebuilding, the B12 is normally considered to be an LNER rather than a GER design.

The B12s were worked hard during the war and after D-day, a number of B12/3s were allocated to American ambulance trains. Their design enabled them to work on most of Britain's railway network, especially in south-west England. Displaced from express services, many found themselves on secondary routes such as the Midland & Great Northern in BR days.

The large-boilered B12/3s were the last to be withdrawn, their last duties being between Norwich and Cromer. From 1959, No. 61572 became the sole survivor, but was kept at work until 1961 by the Norwich shedmaster Bill Harvey, who also resisted requests to send it to Stratford for scrapping.

The Midland & Great Northern Joint Railway Society was formed to save a section of the M&GN which had been closed virtually in its entirety in 1959; the country's biggest railway closure to date. The society was able to purchase its first two locomotives in 1962: No. 61572, the last surviving inside-cylindered 4-6-0, and GER J15 0-6-0 No. 65462, they were moved via Stratford for storage at the LMR's Devons Road diesel depot in East London.

To raise funds to repay a loan which had been taken out to secure the B12, the society put forward the idea of using the B12 to haul a railtour, the route chosen taking it from Broad Street to Stratford-upon-Avon. With a steam ban by then effectively in force on the ER south of March, the route was largely on LMR metals. The proposal was put verbally to the traffic manager's office at Euston and accepted. The engine had in fact been sold by the Eastern Region 12 months earlier but the LMR was not to know that and apparently never asked the question, although the fact that it was no longer a BR engine apparently did start to emerge once the tour was under way.

BELOW: No. 61572 heads a goods train near Ewood Bridge on the East Lancashire Railway.

No. 8572 departs from Weybourne on the North Norfolk Railway with Gresley Quad-Art stock on March11, 2012 .

No. 61572 was towed from Devons Road to Willesden a few days earlier to be prepared for its trip. The aptly named 'Wandering 1500' tour departed from Broad Street at 9.20am on October 5, 1963, with a Willesden crew, running via the GN main line to Hitchin, then Bedford, Northampton and Fenny Compton to Stratford. The return journey was via Leamington Spa to Rugby Midland for a dash up the West Coast Main Line to Watford Junction, Willesden, Camden and Dalston Junction, arriving at Broad Street more than two hours late.

The engine behaved impeccably and a few hundred pounds' profit was made by the society which all helped towards the preservation of the engine. It had become the fourth privately preserved steam engine to operate on BR – all of them LNER engines. It would be 32 years before it was steamed again.

In 1964, the Sheringham to Melton Constable section of the M&GN was closed by BR, and the M&GN Society set its sights on preserving the line running west from Sheringham. After a period in store at March, its two locomotives arrived at Sheringham on June 6, 1967. The B12 was eventually given a major overhaul in Germany before entering service on the North Norfolk Railway in 1995, immaculate in LNER apple green livery as No. 8572.

The engine reverted to its BR identity as No. 61572 in 1999 and ran until 2005, after which it had a further major overhaul with much of the work carried out at Riley & Son Engineering at Bury. It was launched back into traffic on the NNR at the March 2012 steam gala back in LNER green as No. 8572, and has continued to pay working visits to other heritage lines.

No. 61572 passes Pinner during a Steam on the Met event on May 25, 2000, running parallel with K1 2-6-0 No. 62005.
JOHN STRETTON

LNER D49 4-4-0 No. 246 Morayshire and Caledonian 0-4-4T No. 419 depart from Darlington heading for Newcastle via the Durham Coast on August 31, 1975.

No. 246 *Morayshire* at Darlington immediately after its participation in the Rail 150 cavalcade from Shildon on August 31, 1975.

D49 4-4-0 No. 246 *Morayshire*

After the Grouping in 1923 the LNER, along with the other 'Big Four' companies found it had inherited a collection of locomotives, many of which were past their sell-by dates.

By 1925, Nigel Gresley started looking at the provision of a new intermediate express engine for the North Eastern and Scottish areas. At the end of the year, Darlington started work on a 4-4-0 design to replace older NBR and NER classes. The first of the new D49 class No. 234 *Yorkshire* emerged from Darlington in October 1927, the first LNER-designed passenger engine.

Powerful for its size, Gresley chose a 4-4-0 rather than an Atlantic, with three cylinders, using his conjugated valve gear as on the A1 Pacifics. In charge of design at Darlington, was chief draughtsman, R J Robson, but he included a mixture of Darlington and Doncaster practices. The three cylinders and steam chest were in one complete casting, following the Darlington practice introduced by Raven on his C7 Atlantics.

A total of 76 engines in three batches were completed up to February 1935. The first batch, the D49/1s, was fitted with piston valves and named after Shires served by the LNER, while the second, the D49/2s had rotary-cam operated Lentz poppet valves. With the 'Shire' names exhausted, the naming policy changed to 'Hunts', after well-known foxhunting meetings such as The Quorn. The final batch, the D49/3s was built with oscillating cam operated poppet valves, which did not prove satisfactory and these were fitted with new cylinders with piston valves in 1938. The class was the last 4-4-0 type to be built for the LNER and used a boiler designed originally for Gresley's J39 0-6-0.

The bulk of the D49s were allocated to Scotland and north-

On its first railtour duty, LNER D49 4-4-0 No. 246 *Morayshire* climbs towards the Forth Bridge near Inverkeithing on September 7, 1980.

east England. The Scottish Area received 24 D49/1s and one D49/3 and most were allocated to St Margaret's, Dundee, and Eastfield, with smaller numbers allocated to Perth and Haymarket. With the exception of transfers from Eastfield to Carlisle during the 1930s, Scottish allocations rarely changed. They were used for main line passenger trains, the St Margaret's and Carlisle ones working the Waverley route, acquiring a good reputation on this difficult passage.

The D49s tended not to be particularly popular locomotives with the Scottish Area engine crews, mainly owing to the poor ride, and draughty cabs. By 1939, most of the route restrictions on the larger A3s and V2s had been lifted and these locomotives had displaced the D49s from their express passenger duties.

The NE Area D49s were initially allocated to York and Neville Hill. Duties included main line services to Newcastle, and cross-country services to Hull, Sheffield, Grantham, and Lincoln. They were also recorded hauling excursion services to King's Cross.

After 1948, BR quickly started to build large numbers of the Thompson B1 4-6-0s which tended to displace the D49s to less-important jobs. Allocations during this period included Pickering, Blaydon, and Selby. Some of the D49s in the Selby and Scarborough areas were even used to haul coal after 1955, a type of work they were never designed for.

Withdrawals from both the North Eastern and Scottish regions started in September 1957 and the last to go was No. 62712 *Morayshire* in July 1961.

As No. 246, it had been completed at Darlington in February 1928 and in LNER days was allocated to Dundee, Perth, Haymarket and St Margarets. In the LNER renumbering of 1946,

LNER LOCOMOTIVE NUMBERING

The LNER inherited 1359 engines from the GNR, 1358 from the GCR, 1336 from the GER, 2143 from the NER, 1074 from the NBR and just 122 from the GNSR. Naturally there were many examples of duplicated numbers and the 126 engines built by the LNER in 1923 used the numbers the constituent companies would have used, with prefixes N / C / E / D / B and S respectively being added to differentiate between duplicate numbers.

In 1924, a system was introduced where NER numbers remained unchanged while GNR numbers had 3000 added, GCR 5000, GER 7000 and NBR 9000. GNSR engines would take vacant numbers at the end of the GCR allocation but in practice had 6800 added. Consequently, for example, GN-designed A1 Pacific No. 1472 *Flying Scotsman* became No. 4472.

LNER numbers remained extremely haphazard though and a partial renumbering by Thompson of GER engines in October 1942 was designed to make the series from 8300 available for his new B1 4-6-0s. In December 1943 a much more sweeping renumbering was initiated as follows.

- ◼ Express engines: 1-999
- ◼ Four-coupled passenger: 2000-2999
- ◼ Six-coupled freight: 5000-5999
- ◼ Passenger tank: 7000-7999
- ◼ Mixed traffic and freight tank: 9000-9999
- ◼ Six-coupled passenger: 1000-1999
- ◼ Eight-coupled freight: 3000-3999
- ◼ Electric: 6000-6999
- ◼ Shunting tank: 8000-8999
- ◼ W1 4-6-4: No. 10000

While more logical, there were major anomalies, particularly that the A1/A3 Pacifics became No. 500-578 and the A4s 580-613, while four of the A4s remained completely out of sequence as No. 1-4. However, in April 1946, to rectify this, the Pacifics and V2 2-6-2s were renumbered again and these numbers were the ones which formed the basis of BR's system when all LNER engines had 60000 added to their numbers. No. 4472 *Flying Scotsman*, by now an A10, had become No. 502 in 1943, No. 103 in 1946 and then No. 60103 on Nationalisation. The now-rebuilt 4-6-4 No. 10000 had become No. 700 and consequently No. 60700.

ABOVE: LNER D49 4-4-0 No. 246 *Morayshire* approaches Cowdenbeath on April 19, 1981.

OPPOSITE RIGHT: In BR black livery, No. 62712 *Morayshire* passes Woodthorpe on the Great Central Railway on October 4, 2014.

Morayshire was allocated No. 2712 therefore becoming BR No. 62712. In 1958 the engine was moved to Thornton Junction but after two years was transferred to Hawick. When *Morayshire* was withdrawn in July 1961, it was loaned to Slateford Laundry in Edinburgh for use as a stationary boiler. This lasted until January 1962 after which it was stored at Dalry Road shed in Edinburgh.

In 1962 a Mr Ian Fraser who had worked on the class of engine at Darlington was taking an interest in *Morayshire* and arranged with BR for it to be moved to Dawsholm shed in Glasgow where the ScR's preserved steam engines were based. On July 21, 1964 the engine was hauled by GNSR F class 4-4-0 No. 49 *Gordon Highlander* to Inverurie works for restoration to LNER livery as No. 246.

ICI at Ardeer was then able to store the locomotive from December 1966 until June 16, 1966, when it then moved to the Royal Elizabeth Dockyard at Dalmeny where it was officially handed over to the Royal Scottish Museum in Edinburgh, which perhaps fortunately has never had the space to exhibit the engine, so it remained in store.

In 1974 the Royal Scottish Museum agreed to loan it to the Scottish Railway Preservation Society with the aim of returning it to steam to participate in the 150th anniversary of the Stockton and Darlington Railway at Shildon in August 1975, running under its own steam from Falkirk with Caledonian 0-4-4T No. 419 and three pre-Grouping coaches.

The engine remained based at Falkirk and was used on several railtours on the main line in Scotland until withdrawn from service in 1983.

The engine was partially dismantled at Falkirk and owing to relocation of the SRPS to the Bo'ness & Kinneil Railway in January 1998 and because of other priorities, overhaul work only restarted in earnest in early 2000. This was completed in late July 2003 in time to participate in the open weekend at Doncaster works. The locomotive became operational on the line at Bo'ness in August 2005, and has made visits to railways south of the border. It is now in the ownership of National Museums of Scotland, and in early 2014 made a first appearance in preservation in black livery carrying its BR identity as No. 62712.

RIGHT: In contrasting shades of apple green typical of Darlington and Doncaster styles respectively, No. 246 *Morayshire* and B1 4-6-0 No. 1306 *Mayflower* head towards Glyndyfrdwy during the Steel Steam & Stars II event on the Llangollen Railway in April 2009.
DAVE WILSON

4wVBT No. 59

The LNER Y1 was a four-wheeled geared steam locomotive type built by the Sentinel Waggon Works and introduced in 1925. The superheated vertical water-tube boiler and the engine were similar to those used in Sentinel steam wagons. There were variations within the class as regards boiler size and fuel capacity and a two-speed variant classified Y3. Fifteen Y1s and 32 Y3s were purchased.

The advantage of the water-tube boiler was that steam could be raised much more quickly than with a conventional fire-tube boiler. The locomotives only consumed about 15lb of coal per mile and the chain drive was useful because it did not produce a hammer-blow to the track – unlike a traditional steam locomotive – and was considered ideal for work in yards where the track was poor. Another advantage was that they could be operated by one person.

Most were withdrawn from service in the late 1940s and 1950s, with just seven surviving as departmental stock in BR days into the early 1960s.

The vertical boiler was cylindrical, with an inner firebox. Coal was fed in at the top, while the grate at the bottom was slightly conical, so that coal fell towards the circumference. Boiler tubes were arranged in a spiral fashion at three different angles, so construction was quite complicated, and Sentinel contracted firebox construction to Galloways of Manchester.

Y1/2 No. 59 became BR No. 68153 but was then renumbered into departmental stock as 54. It worked all its life at the

Faverdale PW yard near Darlington and was purchased by the Middleton Railway on withdrawal, arriving there in September 1961. It is the only surviving ex-LNER Sentinel Y1 but an identical engine once owned by the GWR survives and there are others around the world, for example in North Borneo.

ABOVE: LNER Sentinel Y1 4wVBT Departmental No. 54 in action on the Middleton Railway in 1990.

ABOVE: LNER V2 2-6-2 No. 4771 *Green Arrow* in Harbury cutting on July 1, 1973 with an excursion from Tyseley to Didcot.

ABOVE RIGHT: *Green Arrow* departs from Sheffield Midland southbound on April 21, 1979.

BELOW RIGHT: No. 60800 *Green Arrow* on arrival at King's Cross from York on February 1, 2003.

BELOW: *Green Arrow* departs from Darlington Bank Top for Hexham via the Durham coast on July 5, 1987.

V2 2-6-2 No. 4771 *Green Arrow*

Nigel Gresley designed the V2 2-6-2 for express mixed-traffic work, and they were built between 1936 and 1944. They were the only major class of 2-6-2 tender locomotives used in Britain.

Obviously a shorter and smaller version of Gresley's A1 Pacifics with 6ft 2in driving wheels, they retained Gresley's favoured three-cylinder arrangement, and 184 locomotives were built between 1936 and 1944 at Doncaster and Darlington works, construction continuing through the Second World War as they proved their usefulness. A further four locomotives, ordered as V2s, were redesigned by Gresley's successor Edward Thompson and completed as Pacifics of class A2/1.

They were versatile locomotives, capable of hauling fast-fitted freights and express passenger trains, but the relatively high 22-ton axle load meant their use was restricted to around 40% of the LNER's territory and could not be used, for example, in East Anglia.

The first of the initial batch of five V2s was built at Doncaster and numbered 4771, emerging in June 1936 and named *Green Arrow*, after the express freight service the locomotives were expected to haul.

In peak condition a V2 could almost match the Pacifics for sustained high-speed running and one attained 101.5mph on a test train. The V2s reputation was more firmly established by its remarkable feats of haulage during the Second World War. On at least one occasion a single V2 hauled 26 coaches from Peterborough to London.

During the 1950s, cracked monobloc cylinder castings became increasingly frequent, but replacement was expensive and in 1956 the decision was taken to replace the monobloc with separate cylinder castings. The 71 engines that were modified, can be identified by the external steam pipes from smokebox to cylinders. In around 1960 experiments were made with fitting double chimneys to two V2s but unlike the A3s, this made little difference to either performance or economy, so although Kylchap exhausts did prove effective, only eight engines were fitted with them.

The V2s were withdrawn between 1962 and 1966, the last ones finishing in Scotland and at York. The last V2 withdrawal was No. 60831 from York on December 6, 1966, the last Gresley engine to remain in service.

No. 60800 *Green Arrow* itself, was a King's Cross engine all its life and was nominated for preservation as part of the National Collection. Accordingly, on withdrawal it was taken to Doncaster and externally restored to LNER apple green livery as No. 4771, the intention being that it would go on display in a new museum to be opened in Leicester. However, in the meantime it was put into store at Hellifield in 1964.

It was moved with three other locomotives to Leicester shed on January 9, 1968, where it remained in store, but with no progress towards the opening of the museum, the engines were moved on to Preston Park in September 1970. A positive turn in the V2s' fortunes came when it was towed to Norwich in January 1972 to be returned to steam by a team led by one-time Norwich shedmaster Bill Harvey. It steamed at Norwich in August 1972 and moved under its own steam to Tyseley on April 5, 1973, from where it made an early return to main line service deputising for a pannier tank in May.

After a more ambitious run to Didcot on July 1, 1973, it ran

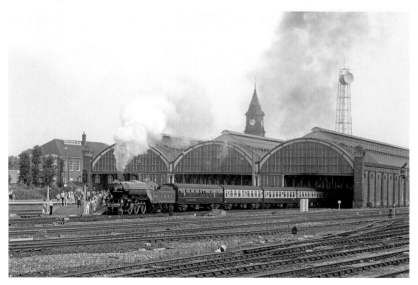

overnight to Carnforth in company with A4 Pacific No. 4498 *Sir Nigel Gresley,* from where it would feature in a number of main line tours, although restricted to the routes to Sellafield and Leeds.

It took some stock from Carnforth to Shildon for the Rail 150 celebrations in August 1975 but returned afterwards to Carnforth. It featured in a Sheffield to Newcastle railtour in September and by the end of the month had taken its place in its new permanent home at the National Railway Museum at York.

From here, its main line career continued and a significant event was the choice of the V2 to haul the first railtour of the Return to Steam programme to traverse the Settle & Carlisle line, in March 1978. Withdrawal for overhaul saw it moved to Hull in 1984 for the work to be carried out by the Humberside Locomotive Preservation Group led by Tom Tighe and it returned to York to resume its duties. It became a roving ambassador for the museum, being seen on the main line at places as diverse as Weymouth and Perth, as well as running on heritage lines including the Great Central, Severn Valley and even the Bodmin & Wenford.

A further overhaul at York paid for by a private sponsor saw an unexpected return to BR Brunswick green livery as No. 60800 in 1998. By 2006 it was back in LNER livery as No. 4771, but it was becoming apparent that its monobloc cylinder casting was showing signs of wear and replacement would simply be too expensive. The option of separate cylinders would not be entertained by the museum as it would destroy the authenticity of a V2 in the condition as designed by Gresley. Although withdrawn from main line use with boiler problems, the museum kept it running by reducing the boiler pressure for limited heritage line use until expiry of its boiler certificate.

A further failure during a high-profile LNER gala on the North Yorkshire Moors Railway in April 2008 appeared to spell the end but No. 4771 was nursed through one final run on the line a couple of weeks later. A firm favourite with enthusiasts for 35 years, *Green Arrow* had become one of the first casualties of the preservation era, consigned to a future as a static exhibit through being deemed beyond economic repair.

ABOVE: In BR green livery, No. 60800 *Green Arrow* is seen near Sheringham on the North Norfolk Railway in December 2004.

BELOW LEFT: Returned to LNER apple green livery, No. 4771 *Green Arrow* departs from Bewdley on the Severn Valley Railway with a train of Gresley teak stock in September 2007.

BELOW RIGHT: *Green Arrow* departs from Grosmont on the North Yorkshire Moors Railway in April 2008.

LNER K4 2-6-0 No. 3442 *The Great Marquess* heads its first railtour on May 4, 1963 past Embsay Junction. GAVIN MORRISON

Newly restored, No. 3442 climbs towards Foley Park tunnel on the Severn Valley Railway on October 14, 1990.

K4 2-6-0 No. 3442 *The Great Marquess*

The NBR West Highland line to Fort William and on to Mallaig is one of Britain's most spectacular railways but presents the operating challenges of steep gradients, severe curves and restrictive axle loading limits. The NBR D34 Glen 4-4-0s were struggling with increasing loads and were regularly doubleheading in early LNER days. Although larger engines could have been used as far as Fort William, it would cause operational problems in that they would not be permitted to run on to Mallaig.

However, with Gresley's GNR K2 moguls being rapidly replaced by the much larger three-cylindered K3 moguls, a GNR K2 was tried on the West Highland by the LNER with considerable success, and several more were moved to Scotland.

Loadings continued to increase and it was intended to accelerate the trains on the line, so Gresley investigated the possibility of producing a more powerful version of the K2. The eventual May 1936 design was for a 2-6-0 with 5ft 2in diameter

coupled wheels, but with three K3 cylinders, a K2 boiler, and a B17 firebox. This would be a powerful engine but still light enough for West Highland duties.

The prototype K4 No. 3441 left Darlington for Eastfield, Glasgow on January 28, 1937 and made its debut on a passenger train on March 4. Showing little improvement over the K2s' performance, Gresley raised the steam pressure from 180 to 200psi to produce a huge increase in tractive effort. The K4 could now handle 300-ton trains with maximum speeds around 60mph on level track while using only marginally more coal with 300-ton trains than the K2s did with considerably lighter loads.

The successful trials led to five more K4s being built. Apart from the prototype *Loch Long* all were named after Highland chieftains and grandees. The K4s were popular with crews but as with all Gresley 2-6-0s it could be a rough ride at speed, and a locomotive designed to climb was not so well suited to the flat straight stretches of the route.

No. 3442 *The Great Marquess* and K1 No. 2005 cross the causeway above Loch Dubh with 'The West Highlander' returning from Mallaig to Fort William on August 10, 1994.

The K4s monopolised West Highland workings but for only 10 years or so until the arrival of the first Thompson B1 4-6-0s in 1947, which replaced the K4s from Glasgow to Fort William following upgrading of the route. These were followed after Nationalisation by an influx of LMS Stanier and BR Standard 5MT 4-6-0s and the new Peppercorn K1 2-6-0s, which left the K4s increasingly confined to goods workings. In fact in 1945, Thompson had rebuilt K4 No. 3445 as a two-cylinder prototype for the new K1.

During the 1950s, the K4s' sphere of operation enlarged and they began to appear at locations such as Edinburgh, Perth, Forfar, Ayr and Tweedmouth. In 1959 all were concentrated at Thornton in Junction in Fife, where their power proved useful for heavy coal traffic but in October 1961, four were withdrawn, with the last K4, No. 61994 *The Great Marquess,* being withdrawn in December that year.

Only six of the class had been built, but the last survivor made it into preservation, thanks to the late Viscount Garnock who bought it from BR and had it overhauled at Cowlairs works and restored to original LNER condition as No. 3442. On April 29, 1963, it hauled a train of new 16-ton mineral wagons en route to its new base at Neville Hill shed in Leeds. It was used on main line railtour work including the doubleheaded run with K1 No. 62005 to Whitby which marked the closure of the lines from Pickering and Scarborough to the resort in March 1965, and a trip from Victoria to Brighton in 1967. It was forced into retirement by the ban imposed on steam working by BR in 1967 and remained in store at Neville Hill until moved in August 1972 to the Severn Valley Railway, where it made a brief return to steam in September 1973.

A start was made on a thorough overhaul in 1980 and the engine entered regular SVR service in April 1988. It was main line certified and took turns on the 'Cumbrian Mountain Express' over the Settle & Carlisle line. In 1989, owner the Earl of Lindsay was in failing health and strenuous efforts were made to get *The Great Marquess* back to the West Highland line for the first time in 30

ABOVE: LNER K4 2-6-0 No. 61994 *The Great Marquess* crosses the Forth Bridge with an SRPS 'Fife Circle' tour on May 18, 2008.

LEFT: No. 61994 and K1 No. 62005 departs from Goathland on the North Yorkshire Moors Railway on October 19 2007 with a rerun of the SLS 'Whitby Moors Special' of March 1965 which marked the closure of the route.

No. 61994 and A4 Pacific No. 60009 *Union of South Africa* depart from Kingussie on the Highland main line with the Railway Touring Company's 'Great Britain' tour, which was steam-hauled from Penzance to Thurso in April 2007.

LNER K4 2-6-0 No. 61994 *The Great Marquess* leaves Bo'ness with empty stock for Edinburgh Waverley on May 18, 2008.

years. It worked BR's 'West Highlander' to Mallaig and its owner was able to travel on the footplate. Sadly he died only a few days later.

The K4 was back on the West Highland in the summer of 1994, celebrating the line's centenary by doubleheading K1 No. 2005 on the first northbound steam passenger train from Glasgow to Fort William since 1963, as well as three doubleheaded runs to Mallaig. The engine remained in the late owner's family and continued in SVR and main line operation, reverting to its BR identity towards the end of its boiler certificate, but it suffered serious damage when a driving wheel slipped on its axle and it was withdrawn from service.

In the mid-2000s, No.61994 was offered for sale and was bought by John Cameron, long-time owner of A4 Pacific No. 60009 *Union of South Africa*. It left the SVR for overhaul by L&NWR at Crewe. Since its latest return to steam, No. 61994 has been kept busy on main line and heritage line duties, including occasional visits to the West Highland line and runs on the Highland and Kyle of Lochalsh lines. It has also gained a reputation for good performances on the heavy Statesman Rail 'Fellsman' trains over the Settle & Carlisle line. ■

LNER LOCOMOTIVE CLASSIFICATION

The various constituent companies of the LNER developed different systems of locomotive classification using numbers and/or letters; but the GER and GCR systems dating from 1856 and 1859 respectively had no real logic to them, while the NBR and GNSR single-letter ones were far too basic. The 1886 NER system of letters and numbers did not always identify wheel arrangements and was applied inconsistently, with for example Raven's Pacifics being class 4.6.2. The GNR system introduced in 1900 did identify particular wheel arrangements by the letter and different types within that arrangement by the number, but was still too basic; with, for example, C1 referring to all 4-4-2 tender engines while C2 referred to all 4-4-2 tank engines. This system was refined by the LNER into the letter and number system familiar today, where the letter denotes the wheel arrangement and the number the individual class.

The letters followed the order: six-coupled passenger, four-coupled passenger, six-coupled goods, eight-coupled goods, small and miscellaneous. Interestingly, although there were thoughts of a 2-8-2 in 1923 and the letter P was allocated, no one seems to have thought there would ever be a 2-6-2 and the letter V in the miscellaneous series had to be used in due course. The number almost always followed the order GN/GC/GE/NE/NB/GNS, and in order of descending size of driving wheel within the constituent company series.

A	4-6-2	O	2-8-0
B	4-6-0	P	2-8-2
C	4-4-2	Q	0-8-0
D	4-4-0	R	0-8-2
E	2-4-0	S	0-8-4
F	2-4-2	T	4-8-0
G	0-4-4	U	2-8-2+2-8-2
H	4-4-4	V	2-6-2
J	0-6-0	W	4-6-4
K	2-6-0	X	2-2-4 / 4-2-2
L	2-6-4	Y	0-4-0
M	0-6-4	Z	0-4-2
N	0-6-2		

There was often a further number for sub-classification. Hence we have Thompson and Peppercorn A2 Pacifics subdivided into A2, A2/1 and A2/2. There were inconsistencies, with some classes having numerous subclasses with virtually no difference between them while some classes containing quite major variations had no subclasses.

OPPOSITE: No. 61994 climbs away from Crag Hall, Skinningrove past Hunt Cliff with the Railway Touring Company's 'Wansbeck' tour on March 30, 2013.
PHIL WATERFIELD

BELOW: *The Great Marquess* passes Winning Junction on the Bedlington/Ashington to North Byth branch with 'The Wansbeck' on March 30, 2013.

CHAPTER 14

A4 Pacifics

They were the fastest steam engines in the world, six of the original 35 engines still exist of which four have been stars of the main line in the heritage era, and in 2013, all six were reunited to mark the 75th anniversary of *Mallard's* 1938 speed record of 126mph on Stoke bank.

ABOVE: In July 1988, Nos. 4498 *Sir Nigel Gresley*, 4464 *Bittern* as 2509 *Silver Link*, and 4468 *Mallard* line up at the National Railway Museum at York.
DAVE RODGERS

The history of the LNER Pacifics is complicated. Gresley built the first ones for the GNR, classified A1 by the LNER, while Raven built some for the NER, later classified A2. The upgraded Gresley A1s became A3s and the streamlined version was the A4. However, when Thompson rebuilt Gresley's A1 No. 4470 *Great Northern*, he kept it as an A1, and reclassified the remaining unmodified Gresley A1s as A10s. No more Pacifics were rebuilt by Thompson but Peppercorn continued to build new A1s and also introduced a Pacific with smaller driving wheels, which he called A2 as the NER-built A2s had all been withdrawn by then.

Although overshadowed by the A4s, Gresley's A3s were very good engines once upgraded from the original A1 design and were further enhanced by the fitting of double chimneys in later BR days. Thompson's rebuilding of Gresley's designs met with little approval but Peppercorn's Pacifics which reverted to Gresley's principles, but were updated to suit very different circumstances, were potentially outstanding, though perhaps lacking the style of Gresley's products.

Peppercorn's A1 Pacifics were fast, powerful, and above all, far more economical to run and maintain than their Gresley predecessors. They suffered from one major flaw however; they were rough-riding and therefore unpopular with crews. They were the obvious choice for heavy trains, but the top expresses remained rostered for the A4s. The Thompson rebuilt A1 and A2 Pacifics were the first LNER-built Pacifics to be withdrawn in the

early 1960s but the other A1s, A2s, A3s and A4s were all rendered extinct at around the same time in the mid-1960s.

Sir Nigel Gresley's A4 Pacifics became legendary as soon as the first one emerged from 'The Plant' at Doncaster. No. 2509 was named *Silver Link;* it was streamlined and carried a two-tone silver grey livery. Nothing like it had ever been seen in Britain. Its appearance alone captured the public imagination like no other steam engine but when it hauled the press run of the LNER's new high-speed 'Silver Jubilee' King's Cross – Newcastle express, and touched 112mph in the process, a new steam speed record, its reputation was secured; the A4s had arrived.

Thirty-five were built between 1935 and 1938, carrying a variety of names, many of which changed during their service lives. Liveries also changed; four were silver, many garter blue and a few apple green, although garter blue quickly became standard.

They got faster and faster; Stanier's competition with his streamlined Princess Coronation Pacifics on the LMS encouraged Gresley to go faster still until on July 3, 1938, No. 4468 *Mallard* touched 126mph on Stoke Bank, a railway world steam speed record that stands to this day.

Naturally the A4s took over the non-stop workings such as the 'Flying Scotsman' from the A3s and the A3s' corridor tenders were transferred to new A4s. Some A4s were also built with new corridor tenders but not all of the class had them and those without did not feature in long-distance nonstop running.

The heyday of the LNER A4s was very short though, as the Second World War saw them painted black and hauling a size of train they were never designed for. After 1945, they regained their status as Britain's top express steam engines, with No. 60007 *Sir Nigel Gresley* holding the postwar steam speed record of 112mph also on Stoke Bank in May 1959.

The Deltic diesels very quickly displaced them from top-link ECML duties from 1961 and the A4s could easily have disappeared by 1964. Fate intervened though in the shape of BR's disastrous decision to use North British-built type 2 diesels on Scottish Region expresses, a duty they were simply not capable of. The ScR A4s based in Edinburgh were increasingly hauling expresses to Aberdeen; the ER no longer needed its A4s and many moved to Scotland where they were extensively used, not on Edinburgh-Aberdeen expresses but on the Glasgow-Aberdeen line, essentially an LMS route, most engines being based at Aberdeen's one-time joint Ferryhill shed.

Two of the King's Cross allocation of A4s entered preservation on withdrawal when 'Top Shed' closed in May 1963; No. 60022 *Mallard* not surprisingly selected for official preservation, and No. 60008 *Dwight D. Eisenhower* donated to a museum in the US. However, No. 60014 *Silver Link* was not preserved, an approach from Butlins being declined by the ER authorities, which did not seem to want to sell it. The 'Indian summer' of A4s on the Aberdeen road that extended the lives of many class members saw them entering the period where the private preservation of main line engines for active retirement was becoming a reality. And if you were going to buy a steam engine to run on the main line, then surely a streamlined A4 is the one to go for.

Of the A4s that ended their careers in Scotland, a preservation society bought No. 60007 *Sir Nigel Gresley*, John Cameron bought No. 60009 *Union of South Africa* and Geoffrey Drury bought No. 60019 *Bittern*, the last A4 to haul a BR train. In addition BR donated No. 60010 *Dominion of Canada* to a museum in Canada. Six A4s survived out of the original 35. Nos. 60007, 60009 and 60019 quickly hauled main line railtours in their preservation careers but enforced retirement soon came as BR's steam ban on the use of privately owned engines took effect from October 1967.

The same three engines played a prominent part in main line steam operations in vastly different circumstances as steam made a comeback from 1972-73 and the first two have been among the most consistently active main line steam engines ever since. *Bittern* though dropped out of the limelight for many years. A highlight was the return to steam of No. 4468 *Mallard* in 1986-88, to celebrate the 50th anniversary of the speed record.

Perhaps even more remarkable 25 years later was the temporary repatriation of Nos. 60008 and 60010 from their North American homes to enable all six surviving A4s to line up together in 2013 to celebrate the 75th anniversary of *Mallard's* record run. Both A4s returned across the Atlantic in 2014.

ABOVE: LNER A4 Pacific No. 60009 *Union of South Africa* at work on the Lochty Private Railway in March 1970. PAUL CHANCELLOR

Back on the main line in Scotland, No. 60009 departs from Aberdeen on March 25, 1978.

Union of South Africa in the process of being dismantled for overhaul at Bridgnorth on the Severn Valley Railway on March 5, 1989.

No. 60009 *Union of South Africa*

No. 4488 had been allocated the name *Osprey* but when it came out of the paint shop at Doncaster on June 29, 1937, it carried the name of the then newly formed Union of South Africa. It was the 11th A4 to be built and is now the oldest survivor.

It was one of five A4s given a 'Commonwealth' name and a modified garter blue livery with stainless-steel trim on the base of the valances and tender. The numbers and lettering were also in stainless steel and the engines were intended to be used exclusively on the six-hour 'Coronation' King's Cross-Edinburgh expresses. *Union of South Africa* was allocated to Haymarket shed in Edinburgh from new and remained at that shed, fitted with a corridor tender and paying regular visits to King's Cross on the nonstop expresses right up until the diesels took over the top ECML services.

No. 4488 lost its valances over the wheels in March 1942 at which time wartime black livery was applied, and its number was changed to No. 9 on January 21, 1946, under Thompson's

renumbering scheme, the number again being in stainless steel. February 1947 saw the engine regain LNER garter blue livery, but all the A4s were renumbered again and had BR blue livery applied after Nationalisation in 1949-50 but quickly replaced by Brunswick green in 1951-52. All the A4s eventually received double chimneys and Kylchap double blastpipes in BR days to make them identical to the last nine of the class built in 1938.

No. 60009 belatedly had its double chimney fitted in November 1958, and on May 20, 1962 finally left Haymarket for Ferryhill shed in Aberdeen where it became one of the A4s which regularly worked the three-hour expresses to Glasgow.

Overhauls still took place at Doncaster and it was the last BR steam locomotive to go through the works there. In recognition of this, on October 24, 1964 it hauled BR's last steam-hauled train from King's Cross, 18 months after the terminus last saw regular steam services.

No. 60009 was one of the last A4s to be withdrawn, on June 1,

1966. Purchased immediately by Scottish farmer and landowner John Cameron in July, No. 60009 was used by BR nine months later on its 'Grand Scottish Tour No. 1' on March 25, 1967, hauling 18 coaches from Perth to Aberdeen and Perth to Edinburgh, assisted by an LMS 'Black Five' 4-6-0. It was then moved by road on April 8, 1967 to work on the Lochty Private Railway in Fife, built by Cameron on three miles of trackbed on his farm, hauling an LNER beavertail observation car.

Changed circumstances saw the possibility of a return to main line use and on April 3, 1973 No. 60009 left Lochty for Ladybank where it returned to BR tracks and from where it was taken to Kirkcaldy to be based in the former goods shed. At first BR would only permit running from Inverkeithing north of the Forth Bridge, to Dundee, but this was gradually extended to cover Edinburgh, Perth and Aberdeen. For many years the only preserved LNER steam engine to carry BR livery, No. 60009 attracted a unique following among steam enthusiasts north and south of the

No. 60009 *Union of South Africa* **heads south out of Glasgow past Neilston on the Glasgow & South Western route to Carlisle on March 23, 1990.**

border on its occasional outings to recapture its former glories on the Aberdeen road.

An unprecedented excursion in 1980 saw No. 60009 heading up the Highland main line to Inverness, a route which had never seen anything bigger than an LMS 'Black Five' in steam days.

After a few years based at Kirkcaldy it moved to Markinch and took up residence in the former goods shed where it stayed until May 1994 with the exception of a couple of years in a shed in the yard at nearby Thornton. In 1984 it finally ventured south of the border for the first time in 20 years, working trains over the Settle & Carlisle line.

In February 1989, No. 60009 arrived for overhaul at Bridgnorth on the Severn Valley Railway, returning to steam in January 1990 and even working on the line occasionally. It returned to Scotland though and continued in main line operation, mainly north of the border. In May 1994 the locomotive left its Markinch base for the last time, on the back of a low loader. Its route took it over the Forth Road Bridge, becoming the only steam locomotive to cross both the road and rail bridges across the Firth of Forth.

Its operating base in England has varied and it has been seen

LEFT: Until 1984, LNER A4 Pacific No. 60009 *Union of South Africa* was not seen outside Scotland and heads east out of Perth over the River Tay on April 18, 1981.

OPPOSITE LEFT: In heritage railway service, *Union of South Africa* departs from Berwyn on the Llangollen Railway on April 4, 1993.

BELOW: In recent years, No. 60009 has been seen in all parts of Britain and here speeds along the London & South Western main line near Winchfield on February 18, 1995.

all over the UK on main line tours and occasional visits to heritage lines. It has since accumulated the highest mileage of any locomotive in the class, and a highlight of its career was in October 1994 when it hauled the first steam-hauled passenger train out of King's Cross since 1969, commemorating the 30th anniversary of its hauling BR's last steam train from the terminus. This event had been made possible by Privatisation and Railtrack's 'open access' policy.

Following expiry of its boiler certificate, *Union of South Africa* arrived at Pete Waterman's LNWR workshops at Crewe in 2010, for an extensive overhaul, returning to steam in 2012, to resume its busy schedule still in the ownership of John Cameron. Runs on the electrified East Coast Main Line remain commonplace with the engine also finding its way to the extremities of the Network Rail system, to Cornwall and Inverness on occasions.

Remarkably on October 25, 2014, to celebrate the 50th anniversary of when it hauled BR's last steam train out of King's Cross, *Union of South Africa* departed from the London terminus once again, heading for Newcastle with the Railway Touring Company's 'Jubilee Requiem' railtour..

Union of South Africa climbs Holloway bank between Gasworks and Copenhagen tunnels, passing the site of King's Cross 'Top Shed' with a Steam Dreams' 'Cathedrals Express' to Norwich on October 11, 2003.

No. 60009 *Union of South Africa* on the 'Jubilee Requiem' is overtaken by a Class 91 No. 91111 at Huntingdon on October 25, 2014. The train marked the 50th anniversary of the same engine hauling BR's last steam train out of King's Cross.

DOMINION OF CANADA

60010

No. 4489 *Dominion of Canada*

No. 4489 was built at Doncaster in May 1937 and was originally to be named *Buzzard* but received *Woodcock* instead and first appeared in works grey livery lined in white, and with apple green driving wheels. It was quickly renamed *Dominion of Canada* in June 1937, being released into traffic in the 'Commonwealth' version of garter blue livery like No. 4488. The coat of arms of Canada was on the side of the cab and a steam-operated CPR-type bell mounted in front of the single chimney.

Dominion of Canada had its valances removed in February 1943 and LNER garter blue livery replaced wartime black in November 1947. It lost its cabside coat of arms and CPR-style chime whistle in April 1949 when it was renumbered 60010 by BR, but the bell was not removed until December 1957 when it received its Kylchap double blastpipe and chimney.

Allocated to King's Cross from new, it remained there apart from five months at Grantham in 1957 and four months at New England in 1963 after the closure of 'Top Shed'. The final allocation was to Ferryhill on October 20, 1963 to be used, along with other displaced A4s, primarily on the three-hour Aberdeen to Glasgow express service. No. 60010 was withdrawn at Darlington shed on May 29, 1965 and remained there in the undergrowth until after the shed closed on March 26, 1966, when it was moved to Crewe works.

Dr Robert Nicholls, the then president of the Canadian Railroad Historical Association had asked BR to donate the engine for preservation at the Canadian Railway Museum at Delson, near Montreal, Quebec. BR agreed to this but would not fund the restoration. Dr Nicholls secured sponsorship from Tate & Lyle, Britain's largest sugar manufacturers, which had strong Canadian connections, and the Port of London Authority, Canadian Pacific Steamship Lines and the Montreal Harbour Board all waived their fees for the costs of transportation. No. 60010 arrived at the museum on April 24, 1967 for an official handover on June 3. However, although occasionally on display it spent long periods in store and its external condition deteriorated.

In 2011 the National Railway Museum in York announced that it would be bringing No. 60010 along with fellow A4 No. 60008 *Dwight D. Eisenhower* back to the UK for a two-year period to celebrate the 75th anniversary of the record-breaking run of No. 4468 *Mallard*. The event would be the first and almost certainly the only time that all six surviving A4s would be together in preservation.

In a huge logistical exercise masterminded by Andrew Goodman of Moveright International, No. 60010 met up with No. 60008, which had travelled from Green Bay, Wisconsin and was shipped to Liverpool in September 2012 from where it was moved by road to the Locomotion museum at Shildon. There, *Dominion of Canada* was returned to its original LNER garter blue Coronation livery with its original number 4489, complete with side valances,

single chimney, and stainless chrome trim, lettering and numbering. It was refitted with a Canadian-style chime whistle, and the commemorative bell that was originally removed when it was fitted with a double chimney but had been sent with the locomotive to Canada.

It lined up with the other five preserved A4s at the NRM on July 3, 2013, and in February 2014 at Shildon.

After this the two North American A4s were covered and moved to Liverpool docks where they were loaded aboard the Atlantic Container Line's *Atlantic Concert* for the voyage to Halifax, where they were unloaded on May 11, to be transferred on to flatcars for onward transport to their respective museums, No. 4489 arriving back at the Canadian Railway Museum on June 4. During the weekend of June 21, the museum placed No. 4489 on display in its Angus Exhibit Pavilion.

ABOVE: No. 60010 on display at the Locomotion museum at Shildon in October 2012 alongside No. 60008 *Dwight D. Eisenhower*.

LEFT: The CPR bell and stainless-steel numerals at Shildon before being fitting to the locomotive.

No. 60010 *Dominion of Canada* in the paint shop at Crewe works just before moving to Canada. NEIL MORRISON

THE GREAT GATHERING

The unique sight of three A4s in steam on a heritage line; No. 60009 *Union of South Africa*, 60007 *Sir Nigel Gresley* and 60019 *Bittern* at Grosmont on the North Yorkshire Moors Railway in March 2008.

Locomotive line-ups are not new but are always interesting and certainly capture the public imagination if several members of the same class can be displayed together, preferably all in steam. In practice, of course, this is not always easy as not only are there very few classes represented by sufficient numbers in preservation but engines can spend several years at a time under overhaul. So, to get all surviving class members in complete condition, let alone steamable, takes a lot of planning and even more luck.

Nevertheless, when A4 No. 4468 *Mallard* briefly returned to steam in 1988 for the 50th anniversary of its record run, the opportunity was taken to line up three A4s at the National Railway Museum, with *Mallard* and No. 4498 *Sir Nigel Gresley* in steam, joined by No. 60019 *Bittern*, not

ABOVE: No. 4489 *Dominion of Canada* on display at the NRM at York in 'Commonwealth' garter blue livery with stainless-steel embellishments, with No. 60008 *Dwight D Eisenhower*.

BELOW: All six surviving A4s at Locomotion, Shildon in February 2014. FRED KERR

steamable but carrying the identity of No. 2509 *Silver Link* in its original livery.

Over the weekend of July 5, 2008, for the 70th anniversary of its record run, *Mallard* was joined by *Gresley* again, plus *Bittern*, now returned to steam, and the fourth operational A4, No. 60009 *Union of South Africa*, but of course this time *Mallard* itself was not in steam. In the same year, the three operational 'Streaks' were united on the North Yorkshire Moors Railway and it proved possible to line them up at Grosmont before the day's running.

Of course there are two other A4s in preservation, and a line-up of all six would be something to see. In 2011, the National Railway Museum announced that it would be bringing No. 60008 *Dwight D. Eisenhower* and No. 60010

Dominion of Canada back to the UK from their North American museum homes for a two-year period to celebrate the 75th anniversary of *Mallard's* record-breaking run. It would be the first and almost certainly the only time that all six surviving A4s would be together in preservation.

Negotiations were conducted in utmost secrecy but obviously involved the owners of the three operational A4s. Luck was on the organisers' side in that in 2013, none of the three would be undergoing overhaul. The North American A4s duly arrived, and so, on July 3, 2013, all six surviving LNER A4 Pacifics lined up in the Great Hall of the NRM, and in February 2014 came together for the last time at the Locomotion museum at Shildon, undoubtedly high points of the LNER steam revival.

DWIGHT D. EISENHOWER

No. 60008 *Dwight D. Eisenhower*

No. 4496 was allocated the name *Sparrow Hawk*, but entered service on September 4, 1937 instead named *Golden Shuttle*. With a single chimney and valances, No. 4496 was painted in garter blue with the stainless-steel embellishments as used on the five 'Commonwealth' A4s were used on the 'Coronation' service. The valances were removed during a wartime general overhaul in January 1942.

After the war the name *Dwight D. Eisenhower* was applied, and on September 26, 1945 No. 4496 was ex-works in garter blue at Marylebone station for the directors of the LNER to view it. The nameplates were covered and it was intended that the future president would attend an official unveiling, but sadly this could not be arranged.

Now renumbered 60008, BR blue livery was applied after Nationalisation but quickly replaced by Brunswick green, and all the A4s received double chimneys and Kylchap double blastpipes like the later-built examples, No. 60008 being modified during an overhaul in August 1958.

The engine was always based at GN sheds, mostly working from King's Cross, but spending periods at Grantham and finishing with just a month at New England before withdrawal on July 20, 1963.

A Mrs Kovacek visited a small museum in Green Bay, Wisconsin in the United States in 1959 and told the chairman of the museum's board that she had seen a steam engine in Britain called *Dwight D. Eisenhower.* Fuller was interested and asked BR if he could buy it. BR said "no" as it still had years of service ahead of it but by the time No. 60008 was withdrawn from service, the Green Bay museum had become the National Railroad Museum, and negotiations with BR over the now redundant engine were successful second time round.

The locomotive was cosmetically restored at Doncaster works and the following spring, it was shipped to the US, arriving in New York harbour on May 11, 1964 and travelling across the US to the museum by rail later that month.

There have been unsuccessful calls to repatriate the locomotive, but in 2011, the National Railway Museum announced plans to temporarily bring the engine home, as part of a plan to reunite all six preserved A4s for the 75th anniversary of the No. 4468 *Mallard's* world record-breaking 126mph run. Both Nos. 60008 and 60010 were loaned to the NRM for two years.

In early September 2012, No. 60008 was moved from Green Bay to Halifax, Nova Scotia, met up with No. 60010 and was shipped to Liverpool, arriving on October 3. Next day, the two A4s moved by road to the NRM's outstation, the Locomotion museum in Shildon.

No. 60008 moved on to the NRM at York where it received a new coat of authentic BR Brunswick green to replace a slightly inaccurate shade applied at Green Bay and in February 2013 the engine was put on display next to sister engine No. 4468 *Mallard.* All six surviving A4s were lined up in the Great Hall for two weeks from July 3, the 75th anniversary of *Mallard's* speed record.

After another line-up, at Shildon in February 2014, both transatlantic A4s were returned from Liverpool docks to Halifax and moved back to their respective museums. No. 60008 arrived at the National Railroad Museum in Green Bay on June 6, 2014, and on June 23, the museum had returned the engine to the display building, where it was officially unveiled as part of a new Second World War themed exhibit on August 2.

No. 60007 *Sir Nigel Gresley*

No. 4498 was the 21st A4 and the 100th Gresley Pacific to be built, released to traffic on October 30, 1937 in the standard LNER garter blue livery with gold shaded lettering rather than the stainless steel embellishments. It was named after its designer in a ceremony at Marylebone, and allocated to King's Cross 'Top Shed' from new. Stainless-steel numbers and letters were applied in January 1939, but *Sir Nigel Gresley* was repainted into wartime black in February 1942, also losing its valances. After the war, the engine regained garter blue livery on March 6, 1947, now carrying the number 7.

Renumbered 60007, *Sir Nigel Gresley* was painted into BR blue with black and white lining in September 1950, but repainted into Brunswick green livery on April 17, 1952. The engine was used for the opening of the Rugby testing station in August 1948, where it was placed on to the rollers without its tender and run up to high speeds to monitor its coal and water consumption. As with the earlier LNER A4 Pacifics, *Sir Nigel Gresley* was built with a single chimney but gained its double chimney and Kylchap double blastpipe on December 13, 1957.

Sir Nigel Gresley is the holder of the postwar steam record speed of 112mph on Stoke Bank on May 23, 1959 and carries a plaque to commemorate the achievement. As with *Mallard's* record, this was descending southward from Stoke Summit, but unlike *Mallard's* run, which was a special attempt, this was with a passenger train returning from an excursion to Doncaster works. The train exceeded 100mph on two other occasions on the same day, and as the nominated member of the British Transport Commission's Eastern area board, Alan Pegler was on the locomotive's footplate that day, though he felt obliged to intimate to the driver that 112mph was plenty fast enough and the engine was eased.

'Top Shed' kept No. 60007 until closure, and *Sir Nigel Gresley* was reallocated to New England on June 16, 1963 but saw little use before being chosen to join other A4s being given a new lease of life in Scotland. It was briefly allocated to St Margarets shed, to work the Edinburgh-Aberdeen trains, until its final allocation on July 20, 1964 to Ferryhill at Aberdeen, where the Scottish Region A4s were being concentrated.

Withdrawn from service on February 1, 1966, it was selected for preservation by the A4 Preservation Society, which was soon renamed the A4 Locomotive Society. The engine was secured,

ABOVE: No. 4498 *Sir Nigel Gresley* **accelerates away from Crewe on its first railtour in preservation on April 1, 1967.** TH SMITH / RAILWAY MAGAZINE

LEFT: *Sir Nigel Gresley* **in steam at an open day at the NCB's Lambton engine works at Philadelphia, County Durham on October 31, 1971.**

BELOW: No. 4498 heads through Calverley cutting west of Leeds on April 30, 1977 towards its new home of Steamtown Carnforth.

and the 'Streak' was moved to Crewe works for overhaul, during which it acquired No. 60026 *Miles Beevor's* driving wheels as they were in far better condition than its own. In LNER garter blue as No. 4498, the A4 emerged from Crewe in March 1967 and after running in on parcels trains, made its first passenger run in preservation from Crewe to Carlisle on April 1, out via Shap, returning via the Settle & Carlisle.

Normally based at Crewe South shed, it made runs on the Southern Region and the East Coast Main Line during the summer but fell foul of BR's ban on privately owned steam engines by the end of October and was eventually moved to a new home at the NCB locomotive shed at Philadelphia, Co. Durham on July 30, 1968, travelling under its own steam via Carlisle.

It was one of the locomotives approved for limited main line running after the lifting of the ban in 1972 and ran from Newcastle to Carlisle in June of that year, followed by occasional runs including one from Edinburgh to Aberdeen. Eventually a move was made to a more suitable base at Steamtown Carnforth at the head of a railtour from York on April 30, 1977.

Carnforth remained its base apart from a period outstationed at Marylebone in 1985, becoming the first steam engine to haul a passenger train into London since 1969.

On the occasion of the 50th anniversary of *Mallard's* record run, on July 3, 1988, the National Railway Museum assembled three of the four UK-based A4s at the museum, the first time this had ever been done in preservation, but this was topped in July

On one of the tours that marked the return of steam passenger trains to the capital, No. 4498 *Sir Nigel Gresley* passes Neasden with a railtour from Marylebone to the Midlands on February 16, 1985.

LEFT: No. 4498 *Sir Nigel Gresley* leaves Selby northbound on September 22, 1984 on what was once the ECML but is now only the line to Hull since the Selby diversion was built west of the town to avoid areas prone to mining subsidence.

ABOVE: Back in BR blue livery, No. 60007 *Sir Nigel Gresley* passes Ewood Bridge on the East Lancashire Railway on February 26, 1995.

With the ECML in the background, *Sir Nigel Gresley* heads a train of box vans at Peterborough Nene Valley on June 17, 1995.

2008, when *Gresley* joined its three surviving sisters in the UK for a display at the NRM.

In 1994, *Sir Nigel Gresley* was repainted into BR blue livery after nearly 30 years in garter blue, and was first seen in this guise as No. 60007 on the Great Central Railway but its normal operating base became the East Lancashire Railway, from where it also continued in main line operation. A highlight of the story of the LNER steam revival was No. 60007's run from King's Cross to Edinburgh on October 4, 1997, for the shortlived but ambitious railtour operator Days Out Ltd headed by Mel Chamberlain.

After expiry of its main line certificate in June 1999, the locomotive spent the summer on the North Yorkshire Moors Railway, where it was found to cope admirably with operating conditions very different to what it was built for. It moved permanently to the line in 2000 and has seen further regular use after another overhaul at Grosmont. It is owned by the Sir Nigel Gresley Locomotive Preservation Trust Ltd and operated by the A4 Locomotive Society Ltd on behalf of the trust, still seeing main line use mainly outside the NYMR's main operating season.

In what is now a common sight, No. 60007 *Sir Nigel Gresley* departs from Goathland on the North Yorkshire Moors Railway, where it made its home in 2000.

ABOVE: No. 60007 departs from Newcastle Central for Edinburgh on September 19. DAVE COLLIER

Sir Nigel Gresley crosses the Royal Border Bridge at Berwick-upon-Tweed with the Railway Touring Company's 'Great Britain IV' on April 16, 2011.

No. 4464 *Bittern*

No. 4464 *Bittern* was released to traffic on December 18, 1937, with side valances and a single chimney and wearing the garter blue livery that was standard for LNER A4 Pacifics at that time. *Bittern* gained wartime black livery and the valances were removed during an overhaul in 1941. It was renumbered 19 on August 16, 1946 under the LNER 1946 renumbering scheme, and served out the last few months of the LNER from March 1947 in postwar garter blue but after Nationalisation in 1948, became No. 60019, being repainted in July 1950 into BR blue, and Brunswick green from February 1952.

Initially allocated to Heaton on Tyneside, it worked between King's Cross, Newcastle and Edinburgh. *Bittern* was once fitted with boiler No. 9025 from the ill-fated No. 4469 *Sir Ralph Wedgwood* after it had been destroyed at York shed during the 'Baedeker' air raid. It was paired with the same non-corridor tender throughout its working life, and allocated to Gateshead from March 28, 1943, it never normally worked the nonstop Edinburgh trains and was a rare visitor to the King's Cross end of the ECML. A double chimney with a Kylchap double blastpipe was fitted on September 6, 1957.

Bittern was transferred from the north-east to St Margarets in

No. 4464 *Bittern*

LEFT: No. 60019 *Bittern* returned to steam for the first time in 34 years at Ropley on the Mid Hants Railway in July 2007.

BELOW: *Bittern* passes Stukeley, north of Huntingdon on April 12 2008 with the Railway Touring Company's 'North Briton' from King's Cross to Kyle of Lochalsh.

No. 4464 as No. 4492 *Dominion of New Zealand* passes Tyseley with an excursion from York to Stratford-upon-Avon on May 12, 2011.

Back in Scotland for the first time since withdrawal in 1966, No. 4464 *Bittern* crosses the Forth Bridge and passes North Queensferry with Steam Dreams' 'Cathedrals Explorer' on May 19, 2012.

Edinburgh on October 28, 1963, but moved to Ferryhill at Aberdeen within a couple of weeks and ran to Edinburgh and Glasgow. *Bittern* has the honour of heading the last A4-hauled Glasgow to Aberdeen express on September 3, 1966 and brought the A4 era to a close on BR. The next day though it hauled a railtour from Aberdeen right through to York and was subsequently purchased for preservation by Geoffrey Drury, a Yorkshire businessman.

No. 60019 initially operated a few railtours from York shed but the BR steam ban curtailed these activities in 1967. It was based at Neville Hill shed in Leeds along with A2 Pacific No. 532 *Blue Peter* from June 1970 and when the BR steam ban was lifted in 1972 managed a couple of railtours on the York/Scarborough/Hull circuit in 1972-73, carrying postwar LNER garter blue livery as No. 19. It was not steamed again after this but was put into store at NCB Walton colliery near Wakefield in October 1974 where its condition deteriorated and it eventually moved to the Dinting Railway Centre along with *Blue Peter* on October 25, 1978.

In late 1986 the North Eastern Locomotive Preservation Group took charge of both locomotives on long-term loan from the Drury family, but while No. 532 was moved to the ICI works at Wilton on Teesside on December 16, 1986 and restored to main line running from December 1991, *Bittern,* which needed major repairs, was cosmetically restored to represent the pioneer and long-lost sister A4 No. 2509 *Silver Link*. It was initially displayed at the Stephenson Railway Museum at Percy Main on Tyneside in this livery.

During a period at the National Railway Museum, York, on July 3, 1988 *Silver Link* was displayed outside with No. 4468 *Mallard* and No. 4498 *Sir Nigel Gresley* to mark the 50th anniversary of *Mallard's* speed record.

On April 28, 1994, the engine was moved to the Great Central Railway in Loughborough for restoration to working order, but this reached only a partial stage of dismantling, and in 1997, the

engine was bought by Dr Tony Marchington, and moved to Southall to join his other locomotive, which was also being overhauled at the time, A3 Pacific No. 4472 *Flying Scotsman*. In 2000, after the over-budgeted £1-million restoration of *Flying Scotsman* was complete, Marchington sold *Bittern* to Jeremy Hosking, who moved it to the Mid Hants Railway in January 2001, for full restoration to finally commence.

On May 19, 2007, *Bittern* was steamed for the first time since 1973, in BR Brunswick green livery and carrying the number 60019. Its first public passenger train for 34 years was the 1pm from Alresford on July 7, 2007, during the line's end of Southern steam 40th anniversary gala. The return to main line action was on Saturday, December 1, 2007, running from King's Cross to York.

It had been a long time coming but No. 60019, which had spent most of its life as a rather scruffy Gateshead A4, and rarely ventured south of Doncaster became a big star of the main line. On July 25, 2009, *Bittern* made a 188-mile run from King's Cross to York nonstop using a second tender, both tenders having corridors to enable a crew change en route just as in the days of the Edinburgh nonstops.

During the winter of 2010-2011 the locomotive was refitted with the valances it had carried while masquerading as *Silver Link* but emerged as No. 4492 *Dominion of New Zealand* in 1937 'Commonwealth' LNER garter blue livery with stainless steel embellishments.

The locomotive was to remain in this identity for three years, but a change of policy saw it revert to its authentic *Bittern* identity but in standard garter blue livery complete with valances. It also made Southall its permanent base and a decision was made to dispense with the use of the second tender.

To celebrate the 75th anniversary of *Mallard's* record-breaking 126mph run in 1938, *Bittern* was specially authorised to make three runs along the ECML in June and July 2013, when it became

the first locomotive in preservation to be officially allowed to break the 75mph speed limit that steam locomotives have on Network Rail main lines. After a night-time test run between Southall and Didcot on May 29, No. 4464 was ready to recapture the glory days of the A4s on the ECML.

On June 29, 2013, *Bittern* set a new record for British preserved steam locomotive speed on the main line, when it officially achieved a maximum speed of 92.8mph near Arlesey on the first of its planned high speed runs. Regrettably the next two runs were postponed several times because of fire risk, but both saw similar speeds being achieved, the last time being on the descent of Stoke Bank on December 7. The engine now carries a plaque in recognition of this achievement.

ABOVE: *Bittern* passes Cholsey on its 90mph test run on the GW main line on May 29, 2013.

TOP: No. 4464 roars through Sandy at 88mph on June 29, 2013.

No. 4468 *Mallard*

No. 4468 *Mallard* was the 28th A4 to be built, at Doncaster in 1938, and is the youngest survivor. It is of course historically significant as the holder of the world speed record for steam locomotives. Carrying standard garter blue livery and with a non-corridor tender,

BELOW: No. 4468 *Mallard* in the Museum of British Transport at Clapham.
JOHN TITLOW

when it entered service on March 3, 1938, it was the first of the class to have been built with a Kylchap double chimney and blastpipe.

The speed record was achieved on July 3, 1938 on the slight downward grade of Stoke Bank south of Grantham, and the highest speed was recorded at milepost 90¼, between Little Bytham and Essendine. The record attempt was carried out during the trials of a new quick-acting Westinghouse brake, which Gresley saw as an ideal opportunity to recapture the speed record from the LMS.

The double chimney and Kylchap blastpipe improved the draughting and exhaust flow at speed. The engine was just four months old, meaning that it was sufficiently run-in, but not too worn. Selected to crew the locomotive on its record attempt were driver Joseph Duddington (a man with a reputation on the LNER for taking calculated risks) and fireman Thomas Bray.

Duddington, then aged 61 and with 27 years on the footplate, climbed into the cab, turned his cap around (as had George Formby in the contemporary film No Limit), and drove *Mallard* into the history books.

Shortly after attaining the record speed, the middle big end did overheat and *Mallard* had to limp onwards to Peterborough. It then travelled to Doncaster for repair.

Stoke Bank has a gradient of between 1-in-178 and 1-in-200. *Mallard,* pulling a dynamometer car and six coaches, topped Stoke Summit at 75mph and accelerated downhill. The speed recorded by instruments in the dynamometer car reached a momentary maximum of 126mph.

No. 4468 *Mallard* passes Neasden and takes the GC/GW route with a dining train from Marylebone to Stratford-upon-Avon on October 26, 1986.

Mallard passes Kettlesbeck Bridge near Clapham, North Yorkshire, with an excursion returning from Carnforth to York on May 16, 1987.

On its last run before returning to being a static exhibit, No. 4468 *Mallard* departs from Haltwhistle on the Newcastle-Carlisle line on August 27, 1988.

On arrival at King's Cross driver Joe Duddington and inspector Sid Jenkins were quoted as saying that they thought a speed of 130mph would have been possible if the train had not had to slow for the junctions at Essendine.

Allocated to 'Top Shed' at King's Cross for most of its working life, it was withdrawn as BR No. 60022 in April 1963, restored to original LNER livery at Doncaster and put on display in the Museum of British Transport at Clapham on February 29, 1964. On the museum's closure, the A4 was moved by road to Stewart's Lane shed and towed to York down the Midland Main Line, to take pride of place in the new National Railway Museum at York, which opened in September 1975.

Although only cosmetically restored at Doncaster in 1963, *Mallard* was not in particularly run-down condition when withdrawn and was relatively easily returned to steam at the museum for the 50th anniversary of the record run. There were no plans for regular long-term main line or heritage line operations and it was only ever intended that the locomotive would undertake a limited series of runs for three years from 1986 to 1988. Its first duty was to haul the inaugural run of BR's new summertime 'Scarborough Spa Express' from York on July

1986, an operation made possible by the reinstatement of the turntable at Scarborough. As a one-off, this train returned from the coast via Hull.

The autumn saw *Mallard,* with Nos. 4472 *Flying Scotsman* and 4498 *Sir Nigel Gresley* on a series of dining trains between Marylebone and Stratford-upon-Avon, followed by a very limited number of appearances in 1987. With the ECML in the final stages of being electrified, BR could not be persuaded to allow the engine to run down Stoke Bank on July 3, 1988 but *Mallard* did at least take over its commemorative train at Doncaster and proudly steamed away from its birthplace that day, covering some ECML mileage en route to York and on to Scarborough.

A programme of tours in the north of England followed during the summer, with the engine working its last train, from Eaglescliffe via Newcastle, Carlisle and Settle to York on August 27, 1988. This last run was somewhat marred by the engine stalling on the climb to Ais Gill with a heavy build up of ash in the smokebox.

On arrival at York, *Mallard* returned to permanent static exhibition and is unlikely to be steamed again, although it has been remarkably well-travelled in recent years, albeit towed, often by another steam engine, to such places as Doncaster, Barrow Hill and even Grantham.

On the weekend of July 5, 2008, for the 70th anniversary of its record run, *Mallard* was displayed alongside the three other A4s preserved in the UK, reuniting them for the first time since preservation. It spent a year at Locomotion, the NRM's 'subshed' at Shildon, arriving behind new Peppercorn A1 Pacific No. 60163 *Tornado* on June 23, 2010.

To top it all on July 3, 2013, *Mallard* celebrated 75 years since achieving the world speed record, and to commemorate this all six surviving A4s were brought together around the turntable in the Great Hall of the National Railway Museum for the phenomenally popular two-week 'Great Gathering'. *Mallard's* two sisters, Nos. 60008 *Dwight D. Eisenhower* and 4489 (60010) *Dominion of Canada*, had been brought over from their respective museums in North America for `this event. ∎

BELOW: *Mallard* **departs from Doncaster for Scarborough on the newly electrified ECML, on July 3, 1988, the 50th anniversary of its record-breaking run.**

CHAPTER 15

Edward Thompson

Much maligned by historians and enthusiasts because of his treatment of Gresley's masterpieces, Thompson nevertheless made his mark on LNER locomotive development in difficult circumstances.

ABOVE: LNER B1 4-6-0 No. 61264 climbs away from Glenfinnan viaduct with West Coast Railways' 'Jacobite' to Mallaig in 2005.

RIGHT: No. 1264 on arrival at Loughborough on the Great Central Railway on December 16, 1978.

In LNER green livery, No.1264 departs from Fort William on June 26, 1999. JOHN SHUTTLEWORTH

Edward Thompson

Thompson was chief mechanical engineer of the LNER from 1941 to 1946. Born at Marlborough, Wiltshire on June 25, 1881, he was the son of an assistant master at Marlborough College, and was educated at Marlborough before studying at Pembroke College, Cambridge, giving him a very different academic background to his predecessor Gresley, who had also attended Marlborough.

After graduation, Thompson worked in both industry and the railways but by 1910 he was assistant divisional locomotive superintendent on the NER, then in 1912 he was appointed carriage and wagon superintendent for the GNR, where he remained for 18 years until he became works manager at Stratford works. Thompson married the daughter of Sir Vincent Raven, the NER's last CME.

Gresley and Thompson disagreed on a number of matters, the biggest being Gresley's conjugated valve gear for three-cylinder engines, which proved difficult to maintain satisfactorily under wartime conditions.

Thompson started a much-needed standardisation programme, which Gresley had failed to do, having concentrated on too many new ideas. Many well-known Gresley designs were rebuilt under Thompson including the P2 2-8-2s rebuilt as Pacifics, some V2 2-6-2s completed instead as Pacifics and worst of all he planned to rebuild Gresley's A1 Pacifics, choosing first for rebuilding, the class pioneer No. 4470 *Great Northern*.

But Thompson's Pacific rebuilds were not good, as they lacked the grace of Gresley's designs. They all retained three cylinders, but now had three separate sets of independent Walschaerts valve gear. Thompson had something of an obsession with having the connecting rods equal in length, and as a result the outside cylinders were placed behind the front bogie with the inside cylinder well forward, driving on different axles. This gave the engine a long wheelbase, causing frequent fracturing of the frames.

The rebuilt *Great Northern* was intended to be the first of a new design of Pacific but the powers that be were not impressed with it and managed to delay progressing the new engines until Thompson had retired.

Thompson improved passenger safety by introducing steel-bodied coaches to the LNER. Until then the LNER had Gresley-designed coaches, the majority of which had teak bodies but by 1940s standards these were considered insufficiently safe in a collision. Therefore during the Second World War, Thompson designed new all-steel coaches that became a forerunner of the British Railways Mk.1 design.

Apart from the solitary Pacific rebuilds, Thompson is noted for having introduced the B1 4-6-0 and its tank engine version the L1 2-6-4T. The B1 proved to be a highly successful design with more than 400 built and two surviving, but the L1 was never popular and was little improvement on Gresley's 0-6-2T on suburban services. The two B1s are the only Thompson engines to have been preserved. Thompson retired in 1946 and died in 1954.

ABOVE: No. 61264 departs from Scarborough on March 13, 2004 with Past-Time Rail's 'Yorkshire Terrier' returning to Doncaster via Bridlington.

ABOVE: No. 61264 departs from Lincoln with the Railway Touring Company's 'Fenman' from Norwich on May 1, 2006.

B1 4-6-0

Thompson designed the B1 4-6-0 for medium mixed-traffic work; the LNER's equivalent to the very successful GWR Hall class and the LMS Stanier 'Black Five', two-cylinder mixed-traffic 4-6-0s and a type of engine the LNER was clearly short of. However, owing to wartime and post-war economies, the LNER, never the richest railway company, had to produce something cheaply and the B1 is a rather more functional design than its LMS or GWR equivalents.

Introduced in 1942, the first one, No. 8301, was named *Springbok* in honour of a visit by prime minister of South Africa, Field Marshal Jan Smuts, and accordingly the first 40 of the class were named after breeds of antelopes, and later acquiring the nickname 'Bongo' after No. 8306 *Bongo*. A total of 274 were built for the LNER and 136 by BR after Nationalisation. Eighteen were eventually named after LNER directors, the class boasting the shortest name given to a British locomotive (No. 61018 *Gnu*).

The B1 was the first two-cylinder main line locomotive constructed for the LNER since the Grouping, Gresley always favoured three-cylinder designs. Construction was slow during the war years and many B1s were built by outside contractors;

BELOW: After overhaul at Crewe, No. 61264 passes Kettlesbeck Bridge on a main line proving run from Carnforth on January 10, 2014.

North British building 290 and Vulcan Foundry 50.

The rather cheap B1s were not of the quality LNER men had come to expect, being frequently criticised for their rough ride. The two-cylinder layout gave the engines good starting power and excellent hill-climbing abilities, but it also caused very bad hunting effects. The LNER needed the B1s though; they filled a gap in the motive power fleet and replaced many life-expired designs.

The B1s operated right across the LNER system; the first batch going to the GE section, where they were an immediate success and were soon working the Harwich boat trains and other top-link workings. They were also popular in GNR and GCR territory and worked most GC line express services, being regularly rostered for the 'Master Cutler' and 'South Yorkshireman' expresses.

No. 61057 was destroyed in an accident in 1950, and the B1's reign on the premier GE expresses was short; being displaced by the BR Britannia Pacifics from 1951. The GE was also one of the first areas to see total dieselisation by 1963. The first normal withdrawal was No. 61085 in November 1961 and the last three B1s were withdrawn at the end of steam in the former North Eastern Region in September 1967.

No. 61264

No. 1264 was built by the North British Locomotive Company in Glasgow and sent to Stratford for painting and acceptance trials, entering traffic on December 5, 1947 at Parkeston Quay shed at Harwich. Its main duties for the next 13 years were hauling expresses to Liverpool Street including the 'Scandinavian' boat trains.

After Nationalisation, the apple green engine was repainted in BR mixed-traffic black and renumbered 61264. It was reallocated to Colwick shed near Nottingham following the elimination of steam on the GE section, but with the rundown of GC services, it was used on fairly mundane duties until withdrawal in November 1965. Along with several other B1s it found a new lease of life as a stationary boiler after withdrawal, but in very run down condition, even losing its centre driving wheels.

On final withdrawal in July 1967, the centre driving wheels were replaced and the engine was towed to Woodham Brothers scrapyard in Barry, South Wales, arriving by April 1968. No. 61264 was the only LNER engine to find its way to Barry, where it kept company for many years with more than 200 GWR, SR and LMS engines.

A group of North London members of the Stour Valley Railway Society had evolved into the Rolling Stock Society and decided to buy an engine from Barry scrapyard. Dai Woodham quoted the group £4500 for his only ex-LNER locomotive and so the Thompson B1 Preservation Society was formed to save it and after years of hard work fundraising, it moved to Loughborough on the Great Central Railway on July 20, 1976, where a long and costly restoration project commenced.

The boiler understandably was the main problem, the firebox being badly wasted, and both barrel and firebox were at one point declared irreparable. It took no less than six years to find a company willing and able to repair it but eventually Pridham Engineering agreed to do the work and the boiler was moved to its works at Tavistock.

The boiler work took 10 years, progressing only as funds became available, but it was returned to Loughborough in August 1995 and refitted to the restored frames in 1996. On March 6, 1997, the B1 as No. 1264 in LNER green livery, moved under its own power for the first time in more than 30 years, and hauled its first passenger train 22 days later. The 21-year restoration project had cost more than £230,000.

Its working life on the GCR was short and it moved to West Coast Railways' base at Carnforth in 1998 to be prepared for main line duties. A Heritage Lottery Fund grant had been obtained to assist with the costs of certification and new driving wheel tyres, and on March 28 No. 1264 hauled a 420-ton train from Carnforth over Shap to Carlisle.

In May 1998, the B1 took part in London Underground's Steam on the Met event, but the boiler still had persistent leaks and had to be returned to Pridhams for remedial work. Back at Carnforth in 1999, it was re-assembled and had another test run, on June 8, 1999 over the Settle and Carlisle line, doubleheading with LMS 8F 2-8-0 No. 48151.

That summer No. 1264 worked West Coast Railways' regular 'Jacobite' service between Fort William and Mallaig on the West Highland Line, and after repainting in BR black livery as No. 61264 for the 2000 season, worked the line for seven more summers, as well as visiting other heritage lines and centres as diverse as the North Yorkshire Moors, West Somerset and North Norfolk railways. With other main line runs particularly on the Eastern Region, it clocked up 1,000 miles on the main line, even finding its way back to its old home town of Harwich on one occasion, as well as King's Cross and Liverpool Street stations in London.

The locomotive adopted Barrow Hill as its home base during 2005, and in 2007, No. 61264 worked regularly on the North Yorkshire Moors Railway, now with through running to Whitby over Network Rail's Esk Valley Line.

With 80,000 miles on the clock in preservation it was withdrawn for its 10-year overhaul in April 2008. The boiler was lifted from the frames by LNWR in Crewe for very comprehensive repairs, while the tender and chassis were returned to Barrow Hill for refurbishment. The boiler work undertaken included an entirely new inner firebox, smokebox, smokebox door, tubes, front and back tubeplates, stays, outer firebox sides, ashpan, throatplate, and one third of the firebox outer backplate at a total cost of nearly £450,000.

Sadly while the locomotive was under overhaul, Bob Mitchell who had spearheaded the locomotive's operations and co-ordinated the support crew, died.

No. 61264 returned to steam in October 2012 and returned to the North Yorkshire Moors Railway, its long-term home, entering traffic on March 2, 2013. It made a main line test run with West Coast from Carnforth to Hellifield and Blackburn on January 10, 2014, and quickly found itself resuming its main line career by doubleheading with an LMS 'Black Five' over Shap.

ABOVE: No. 61264 running as No. 61002 _Impala_ departs from Whitby on May 6, 2013. No. 61002 is thought to be the last B1 to work over the line before its closure.

ABOVE: No. 1306 *Mayflower* and A3 Pacific No. 4472 *Flying Scotsman* cross Eskmeals viaduct on the Cumbrian Coast line on May 8, 1976.

BELOW: No. 1306 *Mayflower* departs from Leeds with a private charter from Carnforth to York on June 12, 1977.

No. 1306 *Mayflower*

No. 61306 was completed just after Nationalisation and emerged in LNER apple green livery and numbered 61306 but with British Railways in cream lettering on the tender.

Associated with Hull Dairycoates shed for many years, it was one of the last two of the class to be withdrawn by BR from the one-time Lancashire & Yorkshire shed at Low Moor, Bradford, at the end of steam on the former North Eastern Region in September 1967. Its last duty was to haul the Bradford portion of the 'Yorkshire Pullman' from Leeds.

Although a preservation society had been formed to save it, No. 61306 was initially purchased from BR in March 1968 by George Priestly, Richard (Dick) Hardingham and others under the auspices of the B1 Locomotive Society, and moved from storage

at Normanton to Carnforth on May 20 that year, together with LMS Fairburn 2-6-4T No. 42085. The B1 was restored to LNER prewar apple green but with its BR front numberplate, returning to steam in 1970, and on May 1, 1971, was named *Mayflower* on the turntable at Carnforth MPD, the name having previously been carried by No. 61379.

It was in the care of Keith Winteringham and Derek 'Pat' Patrick, before being subsequently sold to Pat Kelly, a Bolton businessman in 1974. Pat took it to BR Horwich works for minor repairs and a repaint into more authentic postwar LNER Thompson apple green as No. 1306 before it reappeared on the main line, working from Carnforth to Sellafield and Leeds in the summer of 1974. It took part in the S&DR cavalcade at Shildon 150 in 1975, and had a moment of glory doubleheading with *Flying Scotsman* from York to

ABOVE:
No. 1306 *Mayflower* and A3 Pacific No. 4472 *Flying Scotsman* pass Aycliffe on the ECML with the 'North Eastern' from Sheffield to Newcastle on September 21, 1975.

LEFT: In a scene now utterly transformed, B1 No. 1306 *Mayflower* and GNR N2 0-6-2T No. 4744 depart from Loughborough Central on the Great Central Railway on May 27, 1979.

ABOVE: No. 1306 departs from Quorn & Woodhouse on the Great Central Railway on February 1, 1981.

Newcastle and back on September 21, 1975. Pat Kelly sold *Mayflower* to Gerald Boden in 1978 after one last main line run on the Cumbrian Coast line before Kelly emigrated to Australia. Gerald was already involved in commercial vehicle preservation but this was his first venture into railway preservation. He moved the engine to the GCR at Loughborough in July that year.

It was returned to steam in 1979 and was a regular performer on the line. For the next overhaul though, Gerald moved the engine to Hull on March 29, 1989 but problems with the site at Dairycoates forced a further move with the engine dismantled, to the Nene Valley Railway on May 16, 1991.

BELOW: No. 61306 *Mayflower* heads a train of LNER teak stock towards Ellerbeck summit on the North Yorkshire Moors Railway on May 6, 2013.

The overhaul by the small but dedicated team was completed at Wansford in 2003 and it worked regularly on the NVR. There were no visits to other railways but in 2008 the engine was moved to the Battlefield Line at Shackerstone in Leicestershire, closer to the owner's home, where it was steamed occasionally.

On Gerald Boden's death, *Mayflower* was moved to the premises of Boden Rail Engineering Ltd at Washwood Heath, Birmingham, where Neil Boden had set up a business overhauling diesels for main line use. *Mayflower* made visits to gala events, at Llangollen and the North Norfolk Railway, reverting to 1948 livery as when it entered BR service, No. 61306 also visited the Mid-Norfolk Railway and the North Yorkshire Moors Railway.

In 2013 it made its way to Carnforth for a main line test run on West Coast Railways' traditional Carnforth-Hellifield circuit but did not make a passenger-hauling debut as expected. However, purchase by Suffolk enthusiast David Buck in August 2014 saw it move to the North Norfolk Railway in preparation for what is expected to be a busy future on the NNR and the main line. ■

ABOVE: LNER B1 4-6-0 No. 61306 *Mayflower* departs from Hellifield on its main line proving run from Carnforth on May 2, 2013.

TOP: No. 1306 *Mayflower* passes Castor on the Nene Valley Railway on April 3, 2003 with a test run following overhaul.

LEFT: Now in authentic 1948 livery as when it entered BR service, No. 61306 *Mayflower* accelerates away from Kimberley Park on the Mid-Norfolk Railway on July 15, 2012.

Arthur Peppercorn

Although he was only in the job for a short time, Peppercorn made a very significant contribution to LNER steam locomotive design and his Pacifics especially have belatedly earned the recognition they deserve.

The LNER's last CME was Arthur Henry Peppercorn OBE, who occupied the post for only three and a half years. He was born in Leominster in 1889 and educated at Hereford Cathedral School, starting his railway career as an apprentice with the GNR in 1905.

He succeeded Thompson as CME in 1946 but reverted to many of Gresley's design criteria rather than Thompson's, unhampered by wartime conditions. Thompson had laid down a strict set of guidelines for the LNER's new Pacifics but when the new A1s were finally designed by Peppercorn, he disregarded virtually all of these guidelines. Peppercorn finished several projects which were started by Thompson, but is best known for the A1 and A2 Pacifics, which were some of the most powerful, reliable and economical express engines to have run in Britain.

On Nationalisation, he continued in the same job for BR, now titled chief mechanical engineer, Eastern and North Eastern Regions, retiring at the end of 1949.

Apart from the Pacifics, Peppercorn's main contribution to locomotive design was the K1 2-6-0, which followed Thompson's earlier rebuilding of a Gresley K4 into a two-cylinder mogul, but did not enter service until after Nationalisation. Only one of his famous Pacifics, A2 No. 60532 *Blue Peter,* was preserved, and a K1, No. 62005, but sadly no A1s.

However, a brand new A1, No. 60163 *Tornado,* built as the next in the class, has been constructed, which moved under its own steam for the first time in August 2008 and is probably now Britain's most famous steam locomotive.

A2 4-6-2 No. 60532 *Blue Peter*

The LNER A2 Pacifics were an assortment of engines, the only common denominator being that they all had 6ft 2in driving wheels, giving greater power than the 6ft 8in of all other LNER Pacifics. Initially Thompson redesigned the last batch of Gresley's V2 2-6-2s and built them as Pacifics, and also rebuilt Gresley's P2 2-8-2s as similar but different Pacifics.

It was Peppercorn who created order from chaos and built a 6ft 2in driving wheel Pacific visually identical to his A1s, as opposed to Thompson's solitary rebuilt A1 *Great Northern*. All were classified A2 but with subdivisions.

No. 60532 was built at Doncaster and outshopped on March 25, 1948 after Nationalisation. The livery was LNER apple green with British Railways on the tender sides.

Initially all the A2s were allocated to English sheds, No. 60532 being at York. However, in the autumn of 1949, five A2s were overhauled at Doncaster where a number of modifications were made, including the fitting of a multiple-valve regulator and a double Kylchap blastpipe and chimney. These five A2s, including No. 60532, moved to Scotland as problems were being experienced with the Thompson A2/2s (which were the rebuilt P2s). No. 60532 was allocated to Aberdeen Ferryhill, with all the Scottish A2s used mainly on express passenger services between Aberdeen and Edinburgh.

No. 60532 was named in the LNER tradition of famous racehorses. Blue Peter III was the name of a horse owned by Harry Primrose, 6th Earl of Rosebery, which in 1939 won races including the Epsom Derby and the 2000 Guineas.

Apart from a couple of engines in the North East, the English A2s were relatively early LNER Pacific withdrawals but the Scottish ones outlived their English counterparts and three survived into 1966, Nos. 60528 *Tudor Minstrel,* 60530 *Sayajirao*

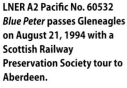

LNER A2 Pacific No. 60532 *Blue Peter* passes Gleneagles on August 21, 1994 with a Scottish Railway Preservation Society tour to Aberdeen.

and 60532 *Blue Peter*. The latter was by then allocated to Dundee and became the last Peppercorn Pacific to be overhauled at Darlington. As a result it was often requested for railtours in its last days, working as far afield as Holyhead and Exeter St Davids, although it came to grief on Honiton bank on the latter occasion.

Its final railtour was in October 1966 over the Waverley route, returning via Beattock. It was withdrawn from service on December 31, 1966 after a paper transfer from Dundee to Ferryhill, and put into store, the last LNER Pacific in service. Although there was a preservation attempt for *Blue Peter,* it was unsuccessful. However, it did result in the engine never making it to a scrapyard and Geoffrey Drury who had bought the last working A4, No. 60019 *Bittern* in 1966, was able to save No. 60532 as late as 1968. It joined his A4 at York in August that year.

After preservation, No. 60532 received support for its restoration on the BBC TV series *Blue Peter,* and the locomotive featured several times in the programme, becoming quite famous as a result. Restoration was undertaken at York, Leeds Neville Hill shed from June 1970 and eventually Doncaster works where it was repainted in LNER apple green livery as No. 532. 60,000 people witnessed its renaming by the Blue Peter programme presenters at a Doncaster works open day.

Its early preservation career was not illustrious. Although it had emerged from Doncaster works to huge media interest resplendent in a new coat of apple green-paint, it was not steamable. BR's steam ban was still in force until 1972 and even then, apart from a period on display at Didcot from May 10, 1972 to April 1973, *Blue Peter* simply remained out of sight at Neville Hill.

It was not until October 1974 that it appeared in steam in public, running with a couple of coaches to Tyseley to star in one of that venue's popular open days. However, it did not return to

Neville Hill; No. 532 and its companion, A4 No.19 *Bittern* were removed from BR premises and went into store at NCB Walton colliery near Wakefield where they presented a sorry sight. It looked as if its day had arrived when it was advertised for a Sheffield-Newcastle excursion in September 1975 as part of the Rail 150 celebrations centred in the North East, but it did not happen for reasons which have remained shrouded in mystery.

A move to the Dinting Railway Centre on October 25, 1978 appeared to mark a possible upturn in the A2's fortunes, and after being tidied up, it was returned to steam in October 1982, but only for very occasional light engine forays down the yard. Much more high-profile was a return to Didcot in May 1985 to take an active part in the Great Western 150th anniversary celebrations but still there was no serious work on offer and it retired once again to Dinting.

But in late 1986 the North Eastern Locomotive Preservation Group took charge of *Blue Peter* and *Bittern* on long-term loan from the Drury family. After a successful fundraising campaign, the A2 was thoroughly restored at the ICI works at Wilton on Teesside, and on its return to steam, this time in BR Brunswick green livery, No. 60532 was renamed by the BBC Blue Peter programme for a second time in December 1991.

It was quickly moved to the North Yorkshire Moors Railway for running-in over the Christmas period and undertook a main line test run from Derby to Sheffield in March 1992, no fewer than 26 years after withdrawal. It became a popular engine on the main line and proved its claim to be Britain's most powerful operational Pacific at the time.

In 1994, during the first run of a preserved steam locomotive from Edinburgh to York since 1967, No. 60532 suffered extensive damage during a catastrophic uncontrolled wheelslip at Durham.

ABOVE LEFT: A huge crowd witnessed the renaming of *Blue Peter* by the BBC TV programme at Doncaster works on November 22, 1970. MAURICE BURNS

ABOVE RIGHT: LNER A2 Pacific No. 532 *Blue Peter* and A4 No.19 *Bittern* in open storage at NCB Walton colliery near Wakefield on January 11, 1976.

Blue Peter **stands outside the Dinting Railway Centre on April 14, 1979.**

RIGHT: No. 532 *Blue Peter* heads a train on the demonstration line at the Great Western Society's Didcot Railway Centre on June 2, 1985.

ABOVE: LNER A2 Pacific No. 60532 *Blue Peter* passes Birkett Common on the Settle & Carlisle line with a NELPG railtour from Middlesbrough on March 6, 1993.

While stopped at the station, the crew overfilled the boiler. As the train departed south across Durham viaduct an initial slip was poorly controlled by the driver, who then reopened the regulator too early, probably worried about stalling on the bank up to Relly Mill. The force of the initial slip caused the boiler to prime, carrying water over into the regulator valve and jamming it open. This allowed steam into the cylinders, perpetuating the slip and accelerating the driving wheels. When the driver attempted to wind the reversing gear back into mid-gear to halt the slip, the force of the boiler pressure spun it into full-forward position, and the driving wheels reached a rotational speed of 140mph before the cylinder heads blew off and the motion disintegrated.

The accident brought to light the importance of train crews being trained on the specific locomotives they were driving, rather than simply a common general instruction on steam locomotives. Neither the driver or fireman had ever worked on an A2 with a multiple valve regulator before, and were unaware of the locomotive's sensitivity to priming, which led to the accident.

The damage to the motion, cylinders and driving wheels was devastating. Moved to Thornaby MPD, the repair work took 18

ABOVE LEFT: K1 No. 62005 stands with GER N7 0-6-2T No. 69621 and LNER K4 2-6-0 No. 3442 *The Great Marquess* in the roundhouse at Neville Hill shed, Leeds in 1967. MAURICE BURNS

ABOVE RIGHT: In apple green livery, LNER K1 2-6-0 No. 2005 shunts stock at Whitby on June 28, 1975.

RIGHT: No. 2005 passes Tees Yard on the approach to Thornaby with a NELPG railtour on October 22, 1978.

K1 2-6-0 No. 62005

As is well documented, Edward Thompson preferred a simple two-cylinder design to Gresley's more complicated three cylinder one. Accordingly he rebuilt K4 2-6-0 No. 3445 *MacCailin Mor* in 1945 as a two-cylinder prototype of the K1 class. Thompson entrusted the rebuilding to his principal assistant Arthur Peppercorn, and when Peppercorn replaced Thompson as chief mechanical engineer, he made the rebuilding the basis of a new class of two-cylinder 2-6-0, but with some modifications.

No further K4s were rebuilt and No. 3445 was based at New England running services usually operated by K2s and K3s. Then, after a period in Edinburgh, it moved to Fort William in 1954 where it remained until its withdrawal in June 1961.

An order for 70 of the new mixed-traffic 2-6-0s was placed

months to complete. The A2 resumed its main line career in November 1996, working a NELPG tour from Middlesbrough to York via Newcastle and Carlisle. No. 60532's main line boiler certificate expired in September 2001 by which time it was again based at the NYMR, where it worked until the end of the 2002 season.

After a period on display at Darlington, No. 60532 was a static exhibit at Barrow Hill. Its owner had died and the Drury family wished to sell the locomotive, which was repainted into British Railways' 1948 apple-green livery and took part in several line ups with various other LNER Pacifics.

In November 2014, *Blue Peter* was purchased by the Royal Scot Locomotive & General Trust, set up by locomotive owner Jeremy Hosking. It will be overhauled at his works at Crewe and return to main line service.

No. 2005 approaches Redcar en route to Saltburn on August 17, 1986.

Temporarily carrying BR black livery, No. 62005 running as No. 62052 departs from Grosmont on the North Yorkshire Moors Railway on September 2, 1984.

RIGHT: No. 2005 rounds the rock face at Lochailort on the West Highland extension to Mallaig on October 16, 1994.

with the North British Locomotive Company of Glasgow, and they were the last steam locomotives built to an LNER design although all were delivered after Nationalisation, entering service between May 1949 and March 1950.

The Peppercorn K1s were seen all over ex-LNER territory but were chiefly associated with the North East and with the West Highland line, with a large allocation also at March.

Before withdrawals started, the K1s started to move away from the GE section in 1958, and by the end of 1961 only eight remained at March. These were moved to Doncaster and Retford by mid-1962, and withdrawals started a few months later. During the 1960s, the K1s tended to take over the work of older 0-6-0 classes.

No. 62005, like all of the class went for running-in to Eastfield shed, Glasgow. From there it went first to Darlington, then Heaton on September 19, 1949, back to Darlington in July 1952, Ardsley in June 1959, York in August 1959, North Blyth in March 1966, Tyne Dock in May 1967 and finally Holbeck in September 1967. The engine had survived until then because it had been used for a brief period as a temporary stationary boiler at the ICI North Tees Port Clarence works.

It was condemned on December 30, 1967 and eventually sold to a consortium of Viscount Garnock, Geoff Drury, Brian Hollingsworth and George Nissen on May 30, 1969 for the boiler

to be used as a spare for the preserved K4 No. 3442 *The Great Marquess* and moved to Neville Hill shed to join the K4.

Ultimately the boiler was not needed for the K4 so No. 62005 was donated to the NELPG in 1972 and it was delivered to BR's Thornaby shed on June 14 of that year for restoration. It returned to steam in 1974 and moved to the North Yorkshire Moors Railway on May 28 that year.

The locomotive had been restored in LNER apple-green livery and numbered 2005. This livery is not historically accurate, as the engine was built in 1949 after Nationalisation. As well as regular use on the NYMR, the K1 quickly saw main line service, on the Whitby to Battersby route on several occasions in the summer of 1975, and made an appearance at the Stockton and Darlington Railway 150th anniversary celebrations at Shildon, along with NELPG's NER T2 No. 2238 and P3 No. 2392.

A further major overhaul took place in 1985 in ICI Wilton Works No 5 depot involving the Manpower Services Commission. It was quickly back at work and by the end of 1986 it had covered 5500 miles on the NYMR and 1067 miles on the main line since the overhaul.

Nineteen eighty-seven saw the engine make its first visit to the West Highland Line, where it worked BR's regular service from Fort William to Mallaig. It became one of the most regular and

No. 62005 crosses the Grand Union Canal near Watford during a Steam on the Met event on May 22, 1999.
JOHN TITLOW

consistent performers on this service for several summers, continuing to also work railtours in the north of England in between its NYMR commitments.

A further overhaul took place and the engine reappeared in BR lined black as No. 62005 in August 1998, leaving Wilton for the NYMR. A rare visit to the south of England took place in May for two weekends running on London Transport's Steam on the Met event, involving four locomotives on a shuttle service between Neasden, Amersham and Watford, repeated the following year.

Returning to regular duties from Fort William, No. 62005 was now under West Coast Railways' banner after privatisation and ran with trains as 'The Jacobite'. The K1 received the name *Lord of the Isles* once carried by K4 No. 61996, though the name is not always carried by the locomotive. Other railtours continued, as did NYMR operations. With the NYMR now operating on the Esk Valley branch into Whitby, in 2005 No. 62005 was able to participate in the commemoration of the 40th anniversary of closure of the line from Grosmont to Rillington Junction. The locomotive had worked the RCTS railtour in March 1965 which marked the closure of the line doubleheading with preserved K4 No. 3442 *The Great Marquess*. On October 20 and 21, 2005, the same two locomotives worked together between Whitby and Pickering once more.

For its size, No. 62005 must be a contender for the title of the most intensively used steam engine in Britain on main line and heritage line services since its return to steam 40 years ago, and there can be few stretches of route mileage in North East England it has yet to visit.

ABOVE: No. 62005 running as Fort William shed's No. 62012 passes Loch Dubh with a train returning from Mallaig to Fort William in October 2005.

LEFT: Soon after leaving Whitby in October 2007, No. 62005 passes under Larpool viaduct which once carried the line south to Scarborough, also closed 40 years earlier.

A rare view of a BR J94 0-6-0ST in industrial service still carrying its BR number. No. 68078 stands at Widdrington opencast coal disposal point in Northumberland.
JOHN SCHOLES

ABOVE: No. 68013, seen leaving Rowsley North on Peak Rail is in reality WD No. 150, Robert Stephenson & Hawthorns No. 7136 of 1944 which was rebuilt by Hunslets with a gas-producer firebox and underfeed stoker as late as 1969 and given a new works number 3892. It was sold straight into preservation at the Dinting Railway Centre.

J94 0-6-0ST

In 1942 the Allied invasion of Europe was imminent and it was decided that it would be wise to build large numbers of standardised and rugged main line and shunting locomotives for use on both British and European railways as part of what was clearly going to be a huge logistical exercise.

Robert Riddles, who had worked with Sir William Stanier on the LMS, was put in charge of the design work, and produced the WD Austerity 0-6-0ST design by adapting the standard Hunslet 18in inside cylinder industrial 0-6-0ST, but with various austerity features as they were not intended to last very long.

Over the four years from January 1943, 377 were built for the War Department by various locomotive builders, and in January 1945, the LNER became responsible for 25 of these engines which had been loaned to the Ministry of Fuel and Power for working opencast coal sites. The LNER conducted formal trials with one and as it needed additional shunting engines, decided to purchase 75 of them which it classified J94 and which were delivered in the summer of 1946. Twenty nine of these were being used by the military in Britain, 40 had been placed straight into storage, and six were under construction by Andrew Barclay & Co.

The LNER modified the engines slightly and allocated them to various sheds mainly in the North East. In BR days they became spread out over more of the NER system but with more now in the northern half of ER territory.

Withdrawals started in 1960 and the last two J94s were withdrawn by BR in 1967 after the last section of the Cromford and High Peak line in Derbyshire was closed. Three had worked on the Cromford & High Peak from 1956 with four more from 1962 but by 1967, Nos. 68006 and 68012 were nominally allocated to the nearest shed with steam facilities, on the London Midland Region at Westhouses.

In view of the success of the design, construction continued for many years after the war with many new engines plus surplus ex-military engines being used in industrial service particularly by the National Coal Board, where many survived well after the end of BR steam. In fact six of the one-time LNER J94s were sold by BR to the NCB between 1963 and 1965 for further service.

Many WD and NCB Austerity 0-6-0STs have been preserved and have proved very useful on heritage lines, having lasted very much longer than intended. No J94s were purchased directly from BR for preservation but two of the class which worked second-hand for the NCB have been preserved, although surprisingly neither No. 68077 or No. 68078 has steamed in preservation. Many strictly industrial engines though have masqueraded as BR or LNER J94s with fictitious numbers in heritage line service.

No. 68077 was preserved at the Keighley and Worth Valley Railway in 1971 but went on loan to the Spa Valley Railway for overhaul in 2005. The work is being carried out at nearby Sellindge. No. 68078 was donated by Derek Crouch Ltd to the Great Western Preservation Group at Southall. ■

BELOW: No. 68030 departs from Sheringham on the North Norfolk Railway. The engine is in fact Hunslet-built Austerity 0-6-0ST No. 3777 which was never in BR stock.

CHAPTER 17

A1 4-6-2 No.60163 *Tornado*

It was the only class of Pacific which ran on BR to be rendered extinct,
but the brand-new A1 Pacific which took to the rails in 2008 immediately
assumed the mantle of Britain's most famous steam engine.

Hauling its first train in preservation, the
grey-liveried LNER A1 Pacific No. 60163
passes Kinchley Lane with a test run on the
Great Central Railway on August 24, 2008.

The first fire has been lit in the almost-complete No. 60163 firebox at Darlington on January 9, 2008. ROBIN JONES

In works grey livery, LNER A1 Pacific No. 60163 in steam for the first time in public at Darlington on August 1, 2008.

No. 60163 sets off from York on its first main line run, with its support coach to Scarborough, on November 4, 2008.

No. 60163 *Tornado* approaches Shildon, hauling A4 Pacific No. 4468 *Mallard* from York for display at the Locomotion museum on June 23, 2010.

It might seem an unlikely thing to do, but a group of enthusiasts came up with a plan to build a brand-new steam locomotive in the 1990s; not a tank engine for branch line services but a Class 8 express Pacific, and the logical choice was the extinct LNER Peppercorn A1. Many said it could not be done but they were to be proved wrong – very wrong!

Edward Thompson rebuilt Gresley's original GNR A1 Pacific No. 4470 *Great Northern* in 1945, keeping it as an A1, and he reclassified the remaining Gresley A1s as A10s. Peppercorn refined the design of Thompson's A1, keeping the same basic dimensions and 49 new A1s were built in 1948/9.

Thompson's rebuilding of Gresley's designs met with little approval but Peppercorn's Pacifics, which reverted to Gresley's principles but updated to suit very different circumstances, were potentially outstanding.

Peppercorn's A1 Pacifics were fast, powerful, and above all, far more economical to run and maintain than their Gresley predecessors, but they suffered from one major flaw – they were rough-riding and therefore unpopular with crews.

The last two A1s just outlasted the A3s and A4s in England, but while everyone seemed to want to preserve and own an A4, no-one was interested in the A1s and Nos. 60124 *Kenilworth* and 60145 *Saint Mungo* went for scrap in 1966, making the A1 the only class of Pacific which ran in BR service to be rendered extinct.

Engineer Ian Storey and colleague Richard Campbell first came up with the idea of building a new express steam engine while working at Carnforth. David Champion had a similar idea and together with Stuart Palmer, formed the A1 Steam Locomotive Trust to do just that in the spring of 1990.

David Champion's idea was that a new A1 could be financed largely by the donations of covenanters; there was enough interest in seeing the huge gap in LNER preservation filled that enthusiasts committed themselves to providing the necessary income stream, matched by generous donations of materials and services by industry. The project was formally launched at York on November 17,

In apple green livery, *Tornado* passes Darnholm on the North Yorkshire Moors Railway with LNER stock on May 10, 2009.

LNER A1 Pacific No. 60163 *Tornado* speeds through Peterborough nonstop with the Top Gear King's Cross – Edinburgh 'Cathedrals Express' on April 25, 2009.

1990, and among those who came on board were PR expert Mark Allatt and aero industry expert David Elliott.

With £10,000 per month flowing in from covenantors who pledged "the cost of a pint of beer per week" each, the frames were cut at BSD in Leeds in 1994, assembled at the Tyseley Locomotive Works in 1995 and moved to Darlington on September 25, 1997, where the new locomotive was to be constructed in part of the NER's Hopetown carriage works near to the Head of Steam museum at North Road station.

With drawings obtained from the NRM and David Elliott acting as director of engineering, construction proceeded steadily and as the unmistakable form of an A1 took shape, the doubting Thomases started to have second thoughts. There was still a boiler to be built and paid for though and for this a £400,000 bond issue was launched in 2004 and the boiler ordered from Meiningen locomotive works in the former East Germany.

This was delivered to Darlington on July 16, 2006, and fitted to the otherwise substantially complete locomotive in June 2007. As soon as Friday, August 1, 2008, this boiler was providing the steam for the A1 to make its first public moves in the siding at Darlington.

Arthur Peppercorn's widow was honorary president of the A1

BELOW: No. 60163 *Tornado* climbs Lindal bank on the Cumbrian Coast line on April 14, 2010.

Steam Locomotive Trust, and at the age of 92, she had lit the first fire in the A1's firebox in January 2008, and was later on the footplate for its inaugural steaming, stating: "My husband would be proud."

After that things continued to happen at lightning pace while the enthusiasts' world and the national media looked on in awe.

On August 24, in grey primer livery, No. 60163 hauled its first train, on the Great Central Railway. On November 4, it took its support coach from York to Scarborough, and hauled a full sized main line test train from York to Barrow Hill two days later, followed by another run, on the ECML to Newcastle overnight on November 18. It was ready for its first public railtour, also from York to Newcastle on January 31, 2009, by now carrying authentic 1948 LNER apple green livery but with BR number and lettering.

A week later, the A1 steamed triumphantly into King's Cross and a hero's welcome, the first member of the class to be seen at the terminus since 1963. This was not a replica A1, this was a new engine and carried the next number in the class sequence. There were a few design improvements; it was an inch lower giving it much greater route availability and attention had been given to the design and construction of the springing, resulting in the engine's riding being nothing like that of the original engines.

The A1s carried names of racehorses, birds, pre-Grouping railways and engineers, with many on the theme of Sir Walter Scott, but the new engine was to be christened *Tornado*, a name decided on after the prominent part played by the aircraft of that name in the Gulf War. It proved to be an apt name and the naming ceremony was carried out by HRH Prince Charles the Prince of Wales at York station on February 19, 2009, after which the Prince and Lady Camilla travelled to Leeds on the Royal Train headed by *Tornado*.

And the achievements just kept coming! Shrouded in secrecy, the BBC staged a race from King's Cross to Edinburgh for the Top Gear programme. *Tornado* did not quite win the race, the vintage Jaguar pipped it to the post, but with Jeremy Clarkson on the footplate, the A1 made Edinburgh in a net time which compared favourably with the schedule for the nonstop 'Elizabethan' in steam days.

The A1 Trust has been willing to repaint its engine regularly. In the first five years we have not only seen it in apple green, but in BR Brunswick green and in BR blue. Apple green was the natural choice initially and it made such an impression that this is likely to be its trademark colour scheme for the future. ■

Now in BR Brunswick green livery and hauling maroon Mk.1 stock, *Tornado* almost recreates the last days of ECML steam as it passes Stukeley north of Huntingdon with a 'Cathedrals Express' to York on March 29, 2012.

ABOVE: *Tornado* passes
Aycliffe north of Darlington
with the Royal Train on July
23, 2012. It had hauled the
train conveying HRH the
Prince of Wales and the
Duchess of Cornwall, from
Kemble overnight to York,
and continued to Bishop
Auckland and Alnmouth.

LEFT: In BR blue livery,
No. 60163 *Tornado* passes
Gleneagles with a
'Cathedrals Express'
returning from Inverness to
London on June 15, 2013.

LEFT: No. 60163 emerges
from Copenhagen tunnel on
the climb of Holloway bank
with a 'Cathedrals Express'
on July 7, 2013. JOHN TITLOW

CHAPTER 18

The future

There is still much to look forward to in the future as the LNER steam revival continues, with representatives of long-lost classes expected to take to the rails.

ABOVE: The working replica of *Locomotion No. 1* in action at its home base at Beamish the North of England Open Air Museum. BEAMISH

The story of the revival of LNER steam in the preservation era is remarkably different to that of the other Big Four companies. No other company had the world's first public railway and its various anniversaries, Britain's first railway museum, *Flying Scotsman*, the world's fastest steam engine, and now of course there is the new A1 *Tornado*.

It did end up though with less locomotives preserved than from the other three companies and *Tornado* has continued a long tradition of trying to fill the gaps, in some cases by building new engines, starting with the working replica of the Stockton & Darlington Railway's *Locomotion No. 1*.

A type of engine perhaps not always associated with the LNER was the Riddles WD Austerity 2-8-0, but many of these did pass to the LNER after the Second World War, becoming Class O7, although in BR days they were regarded as one of the Standard classes and numbered in the 90000 series.

Although they were a common sight in many areas until 1967, the class was rendered extinct in Britain, although some survived in Europe. One, No. 1931, was repatriated from Sweden by the Keighley & Worth Valley Railway and in recent years has reverted from its modified Swedish appearance to BR condition as No. 90733.

Prior to the LNER's use of the WD 2-8-0s, a number of its US counterparts, the USATC S160 2-8-0s, ran in LNER service en route to Europe and these engines found themselves in all parts of the world, several now having been imported to Britain recently and returned to service.

On the debit side, one LNER engine has been all but scrapped in 2014. Doncaster built a batch of LMS 8F 2-8-0s for the War Department during the Second World War and these briefly ran on the LNER, classified O6. One of the batch, No. 48518 found its way to Barry scrapyard and was one of the last engines to be purchased, moving to Cardiff Bute Street in 1988 and back to Barry, but for storage in the locomotive shed at the then Vale of Glamorgan Railway.

It was sold and moved to Llangollen where it has donated its boiler to the new-build GWR County project, with other parts going to the new-build LMS Patriot 4-6-0 project. What remains could still be restored as an LNER 8F but this must be considered unlikely.

While *Tornado* is the high-profile new-build steam locomotive, there are several other projects which are meeting with differing degrees of success. Great Northern Steam in Darlington has made good progress with a new NER 0-4-4T (LNER / BR G5) and subject to funding we can expect to see this running in the future. Progress with a GER 2-4-2T (LNER / BR F5)